In the same series:

ANATOLIA I (3rd and 2nd millennium B.C.)	U. Bahadır Alkım, Professor at the University of Istanbul
ANATOLIA II (1st Millennium B.C. to the end of the Roman period)	Henri Metzger, Professor at the University of Lyons
CENTRAL ASIA	Aleksandr Belenitsky, Professor at the Archaeological Institute of Leningrad
CYPRUS	Vassos Karageorghis, Director of the Archaeological Museum, Nicosia
THE ETRUSCANS	Raymond Bloch, Professor at the Sorbonne, Paris
INDIA	Maurizio Taddei, Inspector of Oriental Art and Archaeology, Rome
MEXICO	Jacques Soustelle
ROME	Gilbert Picard, Professor at the Sorbonne, Paris
SOUTH SIBERIA	Mikhail Gryaznov, Professor at the Archaeological Institute, Leningrad
URARTU	Boris Piotrovsky, Director of the Hermitage Museum, Leningrad

ANCIENT CIVILIZATIONS

Series prepared under the direction
of Jean Marcadé, Professor of Archaeology
at the University of Bordeaux

JACQUES SOUSTELLE

MEXICO

Translated from the French by JAMES HOGARTH

79 illustrations in colour; 105 illustrations in black and white

BARRIE & ROCKLIFF: THE CRESSET PRESS, LONDON

First published in Great Britain by
Barrie & Rockliff: The Cresset Press
2 Clement's Inn, London WC2
Printed in Switzerland

CONTENTS

PREFACE

And so this series brings us to Mexico. The present state of archaeological research in this part of the American continent deserves particular attention. The pattern of Mexican archaeology is an unusual one, for the Conquistadors came into contact with the living traditions of a distant past, and the first historical enquiries into this past were undertaken at a time when a relentless desire to destroy paganism led to the destruction of the most striking monuments of earlier civilisations. Moreover the beginnings of archaeology in the proper sense of the term were hindered by the strong individuality of an art which was disconcerting to the European mind and therefore was for long not appreciated at its true worth, by the distances involved, and by the vicissitudes of politics. Mexican archaeology is a difficult field, and one which is continually expanding in time and space. The discovery of Tepexpán Man has taken us back fifteen or twenty thousand years before our era, and it is clear that throughout the ages a great variety of civilisations, widely divergent in resources, have lived out their span in this large territory, continually developing, influencing one another, supplanting one another or living peaceably together: "At the beginning of the 16th century the Aztec cities, the villages of the north-west and the hunting tribes of the north lived side by side, rather as if, on our own continent, the Romans, the Neolithic inhabitants of the lake villages and the cave dwellers of the Dordogne had all been living at the same time."

The study of stratigraphic data and the establishment of a relative chronology are exciting tasks in themselves; but the advance from a relative to an absolute chronology is no less enthralling. At this point we come up against the problem of deciphering a system of writing which is excellently adapted for the recording of dates or astronomical data but involves computations on a vigesimal basis within a system of cycles which considerably complicate the interpretation of the records. Thus epigraphy and linguistics are clearly of fundamental importance, whether we are dealing with the Maya hieroglyphics or the Aztec pictograms and ideograms. From the cultural point of view, too, as Seler has shown, the myths of Mexico reflect not only cosmo-

logical and theological conceptions but also certain historical events. Accordingly we need all the help we can get from a wide range of sciences and technical skills if we are to fit into a comprehensible pattern all the variety of material remains—beautiful, interesting and peculiarly impressive as so many of them are—which have given the arts of ancient Mexico the world-wide fame they enjoy today.

The problems, the methods and the results of present-day Mexican archaeology are still little known to the general public; and they are set out in this book with an authority and a clarity which the reader will at once recognise.

J.M.

We should like to express our gratitude to His Excellency Sr Agustin Yanes, Minister of National Education of the United States of Mexico, and His Excellency Sr Agustin Salvat, Minister of Tourism, for their help and support during the preparation of this work.

Our thanks are also due to the many individuals and bodies who have given assistance in the task of assembling the illustrations: Sr Ignacio Bernal, Director of the National Museum of Anthropology, Mexico City; Sr Eusebio Davalos Hurtado, Director of the Institute of Anthropology and History, Mexico City; Sig. Guglielmo Manfré, Director of the University Library, Bologna; M. Henri Lehmann, Assistant Director of the Musée de l'Homme, Paris; M. Jean Sirol, Press Counsellor in the French Embassy in Mexico; Mr Gordon D. Gibson, Head of the Department of Anthropology, Smithsonian Institution, Washington; Sra Amalia Cardos de Méndes, Chief Librarian of the National Museum of Anthropology, Mexico City: Herr Lemperle, Principal Keeper, Württembergisches Landesmuseum, Stuttgart; Mme J. Soustelle, attached to the Centre National de la Recherche Scientifique as a research student and to the Department of American Studies, Musée de l'Homme; M. Y. Laplaze, Director of the Photographic Library, Musée de l'Homme, Paris; Miss Dudley T. Easby, Keeper, Brooklyn Museum, New York; Miss Katherine B. Edsall, Keeper, Peabody Museum, Cambridge, Mass.; Miss Elizabeth P. Benson, Curator of the Pre-Columbian Collection, Dumbarton Oaks, Washington; Heer T.J.J. Leyenaar, Keeper, Rijksmuseum voor Volkenkunde, Leyden; M. Priou, Director, Library of the National Assembly, Paris; Miss Nona D.S. Martin, Assistant, Oxford University Library; M. A. Jeanneret, Assistant, Museum für Völkerkunde, Basle; and the American Museum of Natural History, New York, the British Museum, the Museum of the American Indian, New York, the Hermitage Museum, Leningrad, and the Museum für Völkerkunde, Vienna.

We should also like to thank those representatives of the Mexican authorities concerned with tourism — Sr Luis M. Farias, Director General, Sr Adolfo de la Huerta, Secretary General, Sr Guillermo Rosaz Velez, Director General of Information, Sr Arturo Ruiz de Chávez and Sr Alberto Tena Gonzales — who have been so generous with help and advice.

THE DEVELOPMENT OF MEXICAN ARCHAEOLOGY

I

The Earliest Evidence

The great civilisations of Iranian and Mesopotamian antiquity had ceased to exist long before modern times: no European visitor ever saw Ur, Lagash or Nineveh when their streets were thronged with citizens. But when the Spaniards seeking to conquer the New World reached Mexico they came into direct contact with a whole series of native civilisations of great diversity and outstanding vigour. Although the Mayas of Yucatán were showing signs of decline, the Totonacs, the Zapotecs, the Mixtecs, the Tlaxcaltecs, the Tarascans and many other peoples were pursuing their cultural and political development—some of them within the Aztec empire, others outside it. The Aztecs themselves were then at the height of their power, and the European invaders marvelled as they gazed on Tenochtitlán (Mexico City), the dazzlingly white Aztec capital, its tall pyramids and garden-crowned palaces mirrored in the blue waters of the lagoon.

We now know, however, that a number of earlier civilisations, extending over something like four thousand years, had preceded the civilisation discovered by Cortés and his companions. Each one had passed through its cycle of development—from birth to full achievement, followed by collapse and then by revival—leaving its remains on the ground or buried in the earth, and leaving in the minds of men a vague recollection wrapped in the mists of legend. Beside the busy cities of the present lay the skeletons of the dead cities of the past.

The Aztecs and Mayas of the 1520s and later years, like the other peoples of Mexico, were the repositories of oral and written traditions which the Spaniards were able to record. The material collected by the Conquistadors and the missionaries, which often incorporates information supplied by members of the native educated classes, is thus of double interest. On the one hand it gives us an account—often detailed, and always lively and colourful—of the Indian civilisations as they were at the moment of their discovery; and on the other, like a mountain torrent carrying down nuggets of gold, it contains a great wealth of information obtained from native priests and nobles, covering not only contemporary life but also their history and their past.

Thus Mexican archaeology began as an ethnographical study, relying for its evidence on direct observation. It was not concerned with building up a picture of a vanished civilisation, but with describing the civilisation which the Spaniards saw before their own eyes. But the presence of these observers and the circumstances of their intrusion rapidly destroyed the very things they sought to describe—an irreconcilable contradiction which is clearly apparent in the monumental work of the first and greatest Mexican ethnologist, Father Bernardino de Sahagún. The work to which he devoted his life from 1529 to 1590, the *General History of the Affairs of New Spain*, reflects not only his deep affection for "his sons the Indians" and his admiration for the greatness of their rulers, the virtue of their priests, the efficiency and wisdom of their government and the purity of their morals, but also his revulsion against the religious beliefs and practices of the people whom he loved so sincerely. And yet as he wrote his great work in the Aztec language, with the help of informants from the ruling classes of the Empire which had so recently and so suddenly been destroyed, he still felt bound to devote all his religious zeal to "delivering the Indians from the Evil Spirit"—in other words, to demolishing the mental and cultural framework which had survived the collapse of the political structure.

The same contradiction is seen, even more clearly, in the soldiers and administrators. Most of them—like Cortés himself—are full of praise for the valour of the native warriors, the integrity of the judges, and the skill of the architects and craftsmen; and yet they felt no scruple in demolishing the temples, melting down the jewellery and burning the palaces which they so much admired.

The case of Bishop Diego de Landa in Yucatán is no less significant. He wrote an *Account of the Affairs of Yucatán* which, though it lacks the thoroughness and perspicacity of Sahagún's work, does to some extent do for the Mayas what Sahagún had done for the Aztecs; and yet this was the same man who consigned quantities of sacred books to the flames and devoted himself with ferocious energy to the Inquisition's campaign against the "heathenism" of the Indians[1]. It is not surprising, therefore, to find him described both as a historian of first-rate importance *(historiador primordial)* and as a cruel and fanatical zealot.

Nevertheless, for a decade or two after 1520 in central Mexico, and after 1546 in Maya territory, the native civilisations, mortally wounded as they were, still managed to linger precariously on. The Indians and Spaniards lived side by side; the conquerors took wives from noble Indian families, and members of these families were appointed as "governors" to rule under Spanish control. Many Indians who had inherited or acquired a wealth of detailed knowledge—nobles, high officials, military leaders, priests, diviners, doctors, scribes—were still alive. Their memories, trained by years spent in the monastery schools of Mexico City, held a great store of information, much of which was recorded by Sahagún and others; but in addition they possessed numbers of valuable manuscripts—historical and religious works, manuals of divination, genealogies and annals—which had been handed down from generation to generation in family archives or in temples. Many of these books were burned—by Bishop Zumárraga in Mexico City, by Landa in Mérida; but some at least eluded the clutches of the Inquisition.

In addition the Indian scribes continued for a time to produce manuscripts; sometimes they were asked to do so by the Spanish authorities,

[1] Landa was in Yucatán from 1549 to 1579, with the exception of the period between 1566 and 1573, when he returned to Spain.

anxious to learn more about the country and its inhabitants. Quick to realise the advantages of alphabetic writing compared with the ideo-pictographic system hitherto in use, Aztec scholars set about transcribing large numbers of ancient works into Latin characters. In Yucatán the priests known as *Chilam Balam* ("jaguar priests") translated into the contemporary Maya language, written in European script, the old hieroglyphic books which had been copied and re-copied by successive generations and in many cases dated back to a remote antiquity.

Thus this period—sorely troubled as it was, and yet so fruitful—provides us with two types of document. On the one hand we have the various "histories", "accounts" and "descriptions", beginning with the letters sent by Cortés to the Emperor Charles V, the detailed and colourful recollections of Bernal Díaz del Castillo, Sahagún's *History* and Landa's *Account;* on the other there are pre-Conquest manuscripts like the *Codex Borbonicus* (Aztec) *(Plate 175)*, the *Codex Borgia* (Mixteca-Puebla), the *Codex Nuttall* (Mixtec) *(Plate 138)*, the *Codex Dresdensis* (Maya); pictographic and figured manuscripts of the period of the Conquest or slightly later, such as the *Codex Mendoza*, the *Codex Telleriano-Remensis* and the *Lienzo de Tlaxcala;* and books written in Aztec or Maya in Latin characters, like the Mexican *Codex of 1576* or the *Books of Chilam Balam*. Other native authors took to writing in Spanish, like the anonymous historian who wrote the significantly named *History of the Mexicans in their Paintings* (that is, in their illuminated manuscripts).

Whether written by Spanish or by native authors, these various accounts and chronicles do not confine themselves to describing the Mexican civilisations as they were in the 16th century: they also record what was then known about their past. The Yucatecs possessed annals which recorded events in rather summary form but with some chronological precision, on the basis of the "*katun* count" *(u kahlay katunob)*—the *katun* being a

2

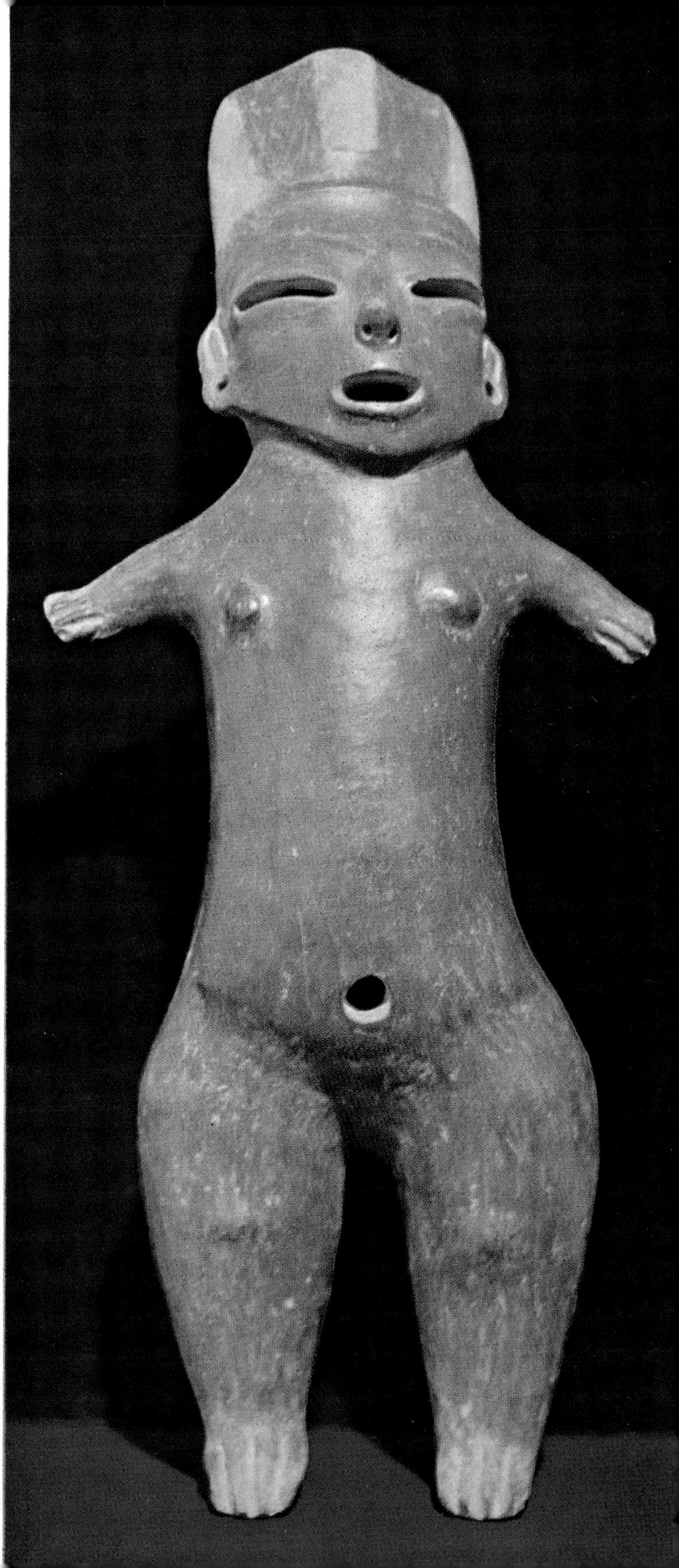

1

3

4

5

6

7 8

9

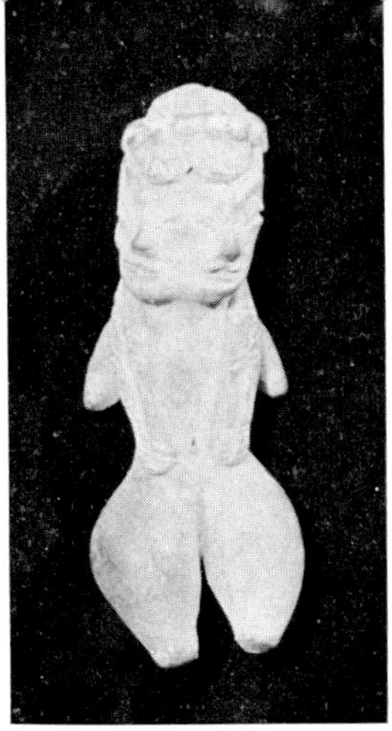

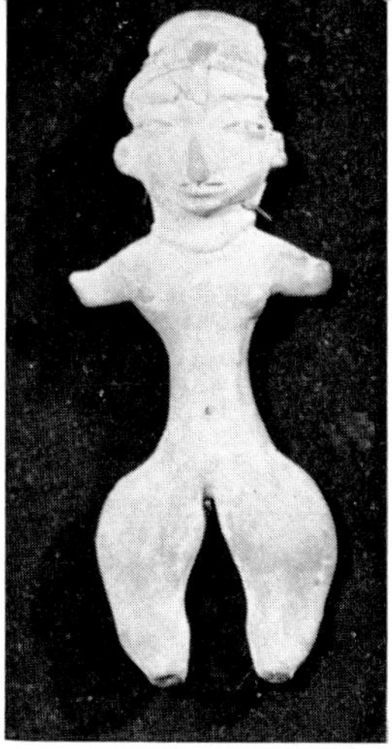

10, 11
12

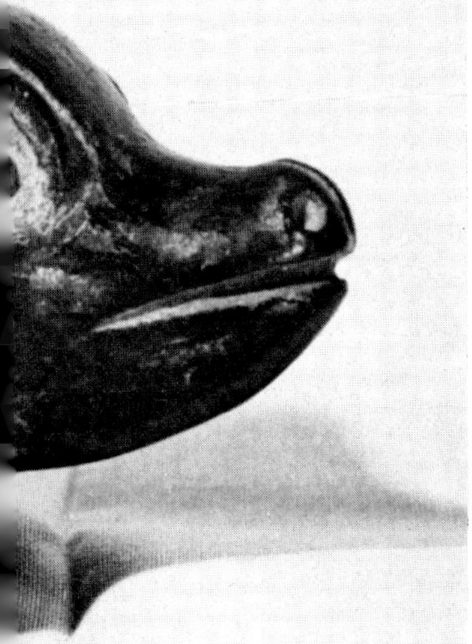
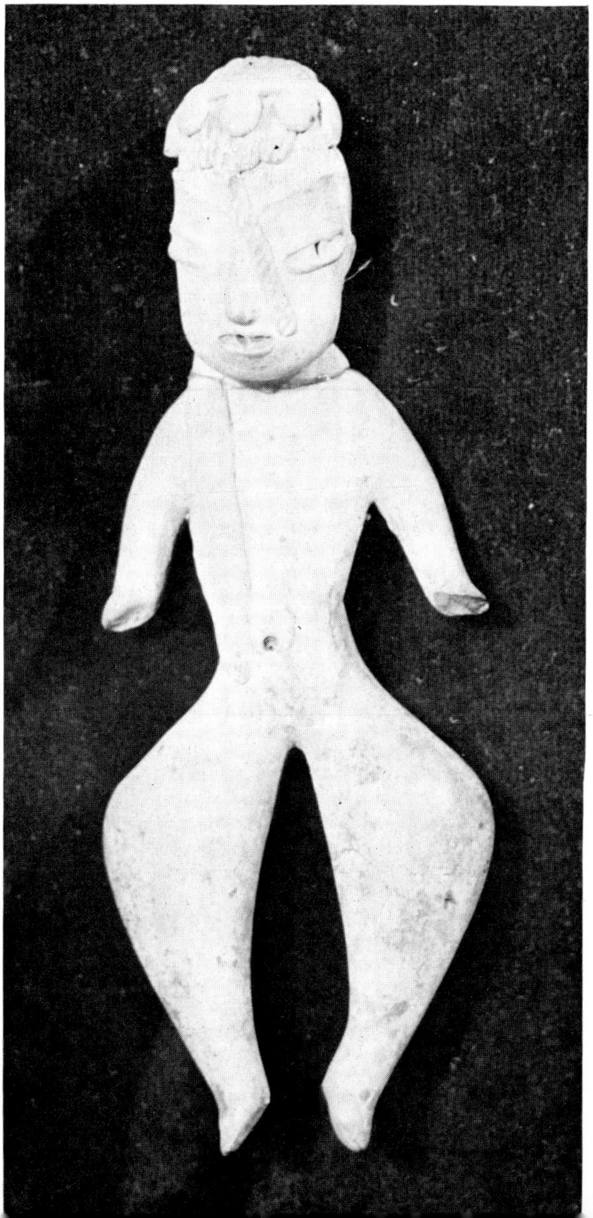

13

14

15

17

16

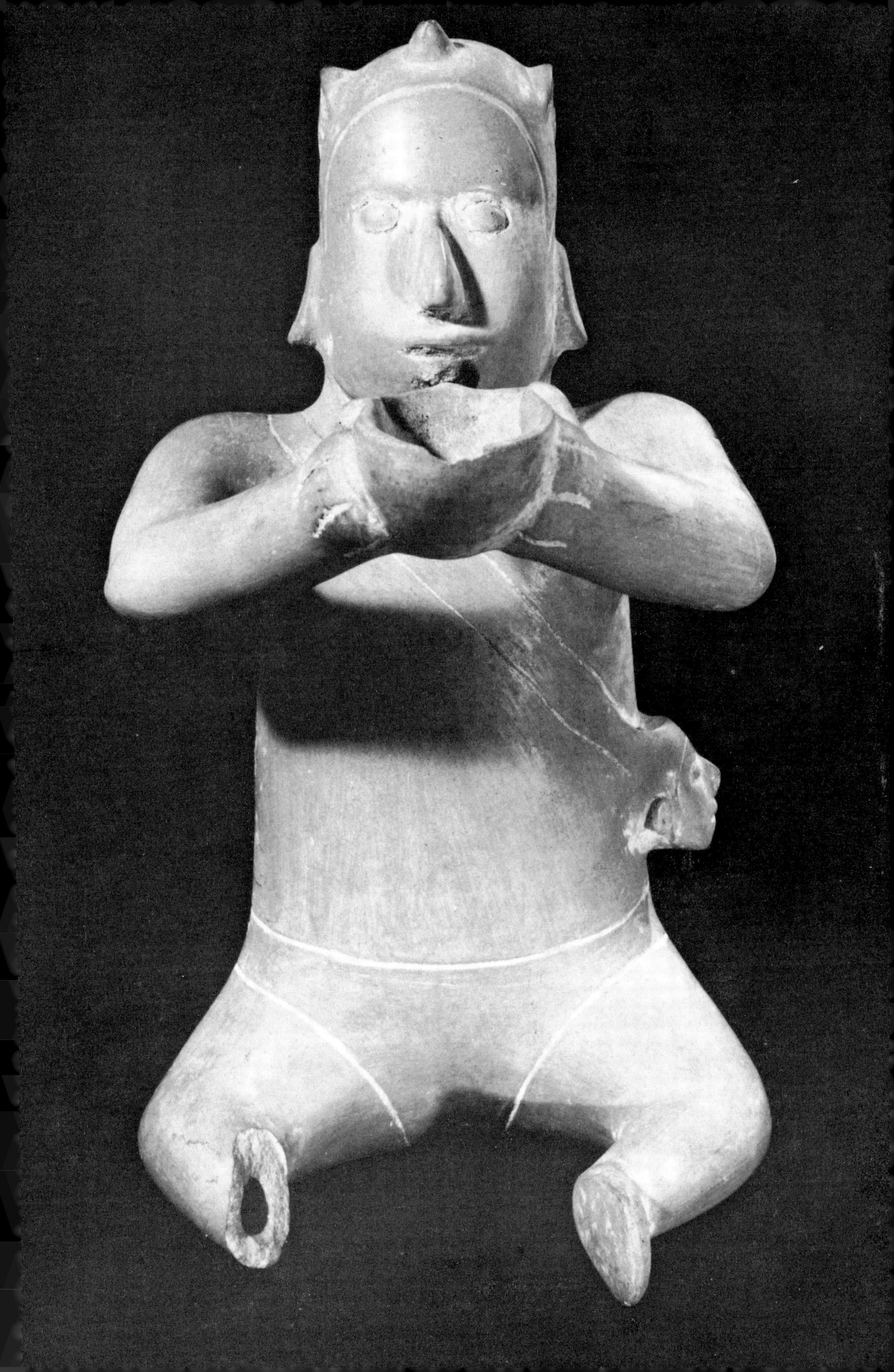

18

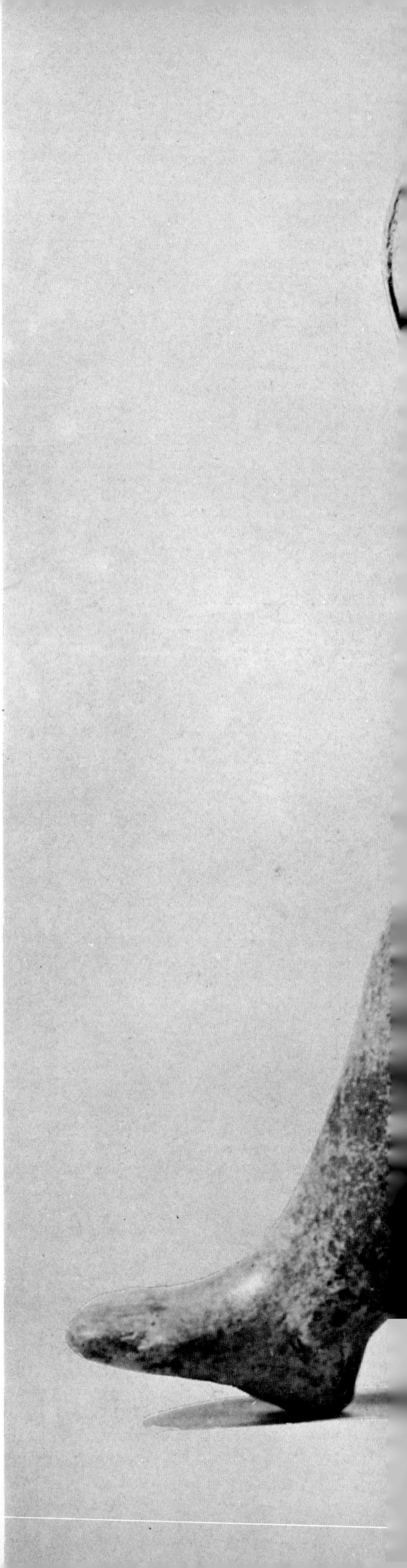

19

20

21

↑ 22, 23 24

↑ 25, 26

very accurately defined period of approximately twenty years. The inhabitants of central Mexico fitted historical or mythico-historical events into cycles of 52 years, so that the same date would recur every 52, 104 or 208 years; but since they noted with great care the occurrence of natural phenomena and the incidents of their life—earthquakes, eclipses, the birth and death of rulers, the inauguration of temples, wars, migrations—we are able to elucidate the uncertainties to which their method of reckoning gives rise. Sometimes veneration for a man's ancestors and dynastic pride pointed in the same direction; sometimes the one ran counter to the other. Thus each royal or noble family sought to trace its lineage as far back as possible, and jealously preserved its traditions; but in the 15th century the Emperor Itzcoatl—in an unhappy anticipation of the Spanish *auto-da-fé*—burned large numbers of manuscripts, allegedly because they gave an inaccurate account of the history of Mexico City, but more probably in fact because they illustrated too clearly the humble origins of his kingdom and his own modest lineage.

Discounting this extreme case, however, we can see that the people of Mexico attached great importance to the records of the past. Their books described the long journey of the Aztecs in their migration from what is now the southern part of the United States, and the arrival of the invaders who came in successive waves and occupied the central plateau, founding the towns of Texcoco and Tlaxcala. They also recounted the history of other peoples, and they were full of marvellous details about the great Toltec civilisation which had preceded the Aztecs and the neighbouring peoples of the same period. This was seen as a golden age subject to the benevolent authority of the god-king Quetzalcoatl, the "Feathered Serpent", the inventor of writing and of the arts, the builder of splendid buildings. Still farther back in the past, the Mexicans believed that their country had been inhabited by giants—a belief founded on the discovery of bones of certain prehistoric animals such as the mammoth.

Farther south, in the mountains of Oaxaca, the Mixtecs—a people gifted with a particular aptitude for the minor arts like jewellery, goldsmith's work, engraving and the illumination of manuscripts—seem to have had the same urge to record their history, and their manuscripts contain an extraordinary wealth of detail for the period from the 7th century of our era onwards.

The inhabitants of Mexico at the period of the Conquest were familiar, of course, with at least some of the great buildings erected long before time. In general they attributed to these monuments a fabulous and divine origin. The Aztecs, for example, thought that the two pyramids of Teotihuacán, some 25 miles from their capital, had been built by the gods themselves. There, they thought, at the origin of the world, when the universe was still shrouded in darkness, the gods had gathered together and had lit a great fire between the two pyramids; and two of them, sacrificing themselves to give light to the world, had thrown themselves into the flames and had then been transformed into the sun and the moon.

But often, too, the Aztecs drew accurate conclusions from what they observed. Thus Sahagún's informants gave him an exact description of the Toltec remains at Tula—the columns in the form of feathered serpents, the tumuli, the sherds of pottery, the vases, and the jade and turquoise jewellery to be found there. Unaccountably, the archaeologists of the 19th and early 20th century consistently under-estimated the importance and significance of Tula until properly conducted excavations showed that the Aztecs had been right.

The situation in the Yucatán peninsula was rather different. Here the Maya civilisation, which about the year 1000 had developed into the Toltec-Maya civilisation, had been in process of disintegration for the past three centuries, the country having been depopulated by a series of natural cataclysms, epidemics and—most disastrous of all—civil wars. The great

Maya towns had been abandoned. Chichén Itzá, from 1000 to 1200 a magnificent capital city, was no more than a skeleton; and Landa describes some of its ruined monuments. Farther south, the splendid cities of Chiapas and Guatemala—Palenque *(Plates 56–66)*, Yaxchilán, Tikal, Piedras Negras—had been deserted for some six or seven centuries and had disappeared under a thick mantle of tropical vegetation, so that the very memory of them had been lost. The same thing had happened in the Gulf of Mexico area, where the buildings and sculpture of La Venta were completely unknown.

Even the most intelligent of the Spaniards had no conception of archaeological research. The buildings of Mexico City had been destroyed by war, the temples ravaged, the idols broken into fragments: now man and the elements were left to do their worst. The *teocallis* (temples) became mere shapeless mounds of earth overgrown with vegetation, a church was built on the great pyramid of Cholula, the ruined buildings and tombs were given up to pillage. Great quantities of stone were torn from walls for the metalling of roads or the building of churches; countless pieces of jewellery, statuettes, and gold and silver ornaments were melted down. This total lack of concern for the remains of the past continued until the end of the 18th century.

But though little interest was shown in the buildings and other material remains of the earlier native civilisations, there were many writers who, basing themselves on tradition and the surviving manuscripts, sought to throw some light on their country's past. The greatest of them, no doubt, was Don Fernando de Alva Ixtlilxochitl, a direct descendant of the kings of Texcoco. His *Relaciones* and his *Historia Chichimeca* are rich mines of information about the history, religion, social structure, laws and government of his city and his dynasty. He wrote in the 17th century, but his work was first published by Lord Kingsborough at the beginning of the 19th century; it was later re-issued by the Mexican government, in a more convenient form, in 1891–1892. Another author was Tezozomoc, who wrote about 1598. Although he was descended from the kings of Azcapotzalco, his *Mexican Chronicle* describes and glorifies the history of Mexico City and the Aztecs. Diego Muñoz Camargo, who was born at Tlaxcala soon after the Conquest, the son of a Spaniard and a lady of noble Indian descent, married a grand-daughter of the last king of Texcoco and was for a time governor of his native province. He died at a great age at the beginning of the 17th century, leaving the manuscript of a *History of Tlaxcala*, written in Spanish, which was published in 1892. A valuable *Account* was also written in 1582 by Juan Bautista Pomar, the son of a conquistador and an Indian lady descended from the kings of Texcoco, where he was born.

If to these works by native authors we add the writings of Spaniards like Gómara, Motolinía, Durán, Veytia, Torquemada, Oviedo and Las Casas, and those of Sahagún and Landa which have already been mentioned, it can be seen that there is an abundance of historical and descriptive literature. But, in all this material, no attention was paid to archaeology in any strict sense of the term.

In August 1790 large-scale operations were undertaken in Mexico City for renewing the paving and drainage of the central square (the Zócalo), and in the course of these operations two carved monoliths came to light—the colossal statue of the earth goddess Coatlicue, the "lady with the serpent skirt", and the large solar disc known as the Calendar Stone. The learned Don Antonio de León y Gama published a detailed description of these objects, with a commentary which shows a profound knowledge—by the standards of the time—of the ancient Mexican civilisation. But what is new and important is that León y Gama, like a modern archaeologist, starts from the object in front of him, submitting it to meticulous examination in order to draw wider conclusions. His book shows that he was aware of the developments in archaeological studies then in progress in Europe: "If excavations were undertaken", he writes, "similar to those at present being carried out in Italy with the object of finding statues and fragments (of sculpture) which recall the memory of ancient Rome... how many monuments of the ancient Indian civilisation should we not find? What treasures should we not discover?"

This seems to have been the first comparison between the ancient civilisations of Mexico and European classical antiquity, and the first formulation—as an objective if not yet as a definite plan—of the idea of excavation for the purpose of extracting the treasures buried underground.

León y Gama's work was not at once published in full, but in 1832 a prominent political figure, Carlos María de Bustamante, undertook its publication under government auspices—a clear indication that wider circles were becoming aware of the importance of proper archaeological investigation. It is likely that Mexican archaeology would have taken a great leap forward at this period, had not an almost continuous succession of civil and foreign wars, *pronunciamientos* and invasions interrupted the normal development of the country and thrust scientific considerations into the background. For years large areas in Mexico and Central America were in a state of such insecurity that any journeys for ethnological or archaeological purposes were exposed not only to difficulties but to grave dangers; and meanwhile it was as much as any government could do to maintain its position in the midst of the continual turmoil.

The Central American Federation formed on the achievement of independence did not take long to fall apart; and its collapse led to a series of bloody struggles between the separate states which then emerged and, within these new republics, between Indians and Creoles, liberals and conservatives, civilian governments and military *caudillos*. In the resultant chaos the Maya territory in Guatemala and Honduras was closed to archaeological research at least as much by man and his quarrels as by natural conditions and climate.

The First Excavations

In spite of all these obstacles, however, the learned world began in the early 19th century to display an increasing interest in Mexican archaeology. The first signs of this interest, indeed, had appeared towards the end of the previous century, when the King of Spain was induced by reports from Spanish travellers who had chanced to observe the ruins of Palenque to send an officer to reconnoitre the area in 1786.

Captain Antonio del Río arrived at Palenque on 3rd May 1787, spent only a short time there—though unfortunately long enough to inflict serious damage on some of the monuments—and drew up a brief and superficial report illustrated with inaccurate drawings. The report was sent to Mexico City, where it aroused little interest—mainly on account of the prejudice then current against the "idolatries" of the Indians—and was filed away in an official pigeonhole. A copy of the report was made, however, and it was published in London in 1822.

Eighteen years after Captain del Río's unproductive expedition King Charles of Spain entrusted a competent officer, Col. Dupaix, with an important mission; and in 1805, 1806 and 1807 Dupaix surveyed and studied the ruins of Palenque in the Chiapas country and Mitla in Oaxaca. He was accompanied by the Mexican artist Luciano Castañeda, who made a large number of drawings. At this point, however, Mexico became involved in the period of troubles during which it achieved independence; and Dupaix's reports and the accompanying drawings disappeared, and were not seen again until a Frenchman, Baradère, discovered them in Mexico City in 1828 *(Plates 56–66)*.

Baradère obtained permission from the Mexican government to take Castañeda's drawings to Paris, and it was arranged that he should also be sent a copy of Dupaix's manuscript. Some years earlier, in 1825, the Société de Géographie of Paris had undertaken to present its Prize to the first traveller who brought back authentic material about Palenque. Baradère had to wait for some years before he received his copy of Dupaix's work; but at last, after every conceivable delay and difficulty, the complete report was published by Firmin Didot of Paris in 1844, in two splendid volumes (including a volume of plates) under the title of *Antiquités Mexicaines*. The importance of the occasion was expressed in a letter from the famous President and dictator of Mexico, Santa Anna, who wrote (6th December 1834): "The temple and other monuments of Palenque may fitly be compared with the pyramids of Egypt."

Another comparison was suggested by Chateaubriand, who wrote on 10th September 1836, after studying the drawings: "Do you not see a striking similarity between monuments of this kind and the monuments of India?" Then, after some melancholy and poetic reflections on "these pompous monuments which once dominated the forests, their fallen walls now overgrown with trees", he went on to compare the Mexican ruins with those of Indochina, China and Egypt.

Earlier still Baron Alexander von Humboldt had taken his place as the first German scholar to concern himself with Mexican antiquities. In his *Views of the Cordilleras* (1816) he referred to the monuments of Palenque and described Aztec sculpture, the pyramids of Teotihuacán *(Plate 41)*, and the monuments of Xochicalco and Mitla.

In 1831, during further work in the central square of Mexico City, another carved monolith was found, built into the foundations of the Palace. This time, however, the extent and cost of the work involved gave the authorities pause: the monolith was left where it was, and was not excavated until 1926. This was the famous "*Teocalli* of the Sacred War", one of the most important works of Aztec religious sculpture[2].

In 1839 John L. Stephens, an indefatigable and cultivated American who had travelled widely in the East, was entrusted by President Van Buren with a diplomatic mission to Central America. All the countries belonging to the Federation, from Guatemala to Costa Rica, were then in such a state of anarchy that the temporary diplomat spent almost two years looking for a legitimate government to which he could present his credentials. Suspected by each faction of supporting the opposing side, sometimes arrested and threatened with execution, often caught up in battles between the contending parties, Stephens remained unperturbed. In conditions of incredible discomfort and danger he travelled extensively in Guatemala, Salvador, Honduras, Nicaragua, Costa Rica, Chiapas und Yucatán in 1839 and 1840, accompanied by the British artist Frederick Catherwood, whose fine drawings, executed with extraordinary delicacy and precision, gave Stephens' book, which was published in New York in 1841, outstanding value as a scientific record. The work was so successful that in the autumn of 1841 Stephens set off again for Yucatán with Catherwood and Samuel Cabot, a doctor and naturalist. A further season of exploration which ended in May 1842 enabled him to describe, among other things, the ruins of Uxmal and Kabah.

With Stephens' work the cities of Yucatán, the sites of Palenque, Quiriguá and Copán, were brought into the domain of scientific archaeology. The same cannot be said of the writings and drawings of "Count" Jean Frédéric Waldeck who, after serving with Napoleon in Egypt and Lord Cochrane in

[2] Other discoveries have been made in the Plaza de Armas and the adjacent streets. In 1897 a carved monolith, the "Piedra de los Guerreros", was recovered from the foundations of the Centro Mercantil. Fifty-two carved and painted stone panels and as many more stones of smaller size were brought to light in 1913 in the Calle Guatemala. Only twenty of the former and nine of the latter were extracted, the remainder being left where they were. The carvings represented a procession of high dignitaries and of feathered serpents; they can be dated to the beginning of the 15th century. Similar slabs had previously been found in 1901.

Chile, spent two years at Palenque recording the carvings, "improving" them in accordance with the neo-classical taste which had been fashionable in his youth. He lived to the great age of 109, when he died—as a result of an accident—in Paris.

This eccentric adventurer was attracted to Palenque by reading Antonio del Río's report; and this report, inadequate as it was, can also claim the merit of having awakened in a young man from the North of France an interest which was to become the ruling passion of his life.

From Brasseur to Aubin

Charles-Etienne Brasseur, known as Brasseur de Bourbourg, came from the small town of Bourbourg near Dunkirk. In later years he claimed that he was able to make enlightening comparisons between his native Flemish, Dutch, and Quiche, a Maya dialect spoken in Guatemala: an assertion which suggests that Brasseur was often governed more by imagination than by scientific argument. But there was no doubt about his vocation. As a boy he devoured every book he could lay hands on which dealt with Egypt, India and Persia, and then took a special interest in the Conquest of Mexico. In 1832, when he was 15, he read a report in the *Gazette de France*—clearly a fabrication—that a tomb had been found near Montevideo containing a helmet with a Greek inscription referring to Ptolemy and a sword decorated with a portrait of Alexander. His attention was now fixed on America; and soon afterwards he read in the *Journal des Savants* a summary of del Río's report on Palenque. Thirty years later he could still recall with emotion "the impression of astonishment mingled with pleasure" which overcame him: the reading of this report, he said, "determined my vocation as an archaeologist". The renown of Champollion, the decipherer of the Egyptian hieroglyphs, was then beginning to spread through provincial France, and the young Brasseur de Bourbourg was fired with the ambition of becoming the Champollion of America.

Coming as he did from a family of modest means, with no resources behind him, Brasseur decided to take orders. Although he himself never said this in so many words, his vocation as a priest seems to have developed. from, and contributed to, his vocation as an archaeologist. At any rate he was now able, as chaplain to the French Legation in Mexico City and as parish priest at Rabinal and San Juan Sacatapéquez in Guatemala, to travel indefatigably all over America, from Canada to Salvador, in four long journeys which were punctuated by stays in Rome, Madrid and Paris.

Brasseur was a great rummager in libraries and bookshops. In Madrid he discovered the manuscript of Landa's *Account of the Affairs of Yucatán* and a fragment of an ancient Maya codex. He bought the manuscript of the famous Motul dictionary of the Maya language for four piastres from a second-hand bookseller in Mexico City but, being short of money, had to sell it for 150 dollars to John Carter Brown of Providence, Rhode Island. In the library of San Gregorio College in Mexico City he found the manuscript in the Nahuatl language which he called the *Codex Chimalpopoca*, containing historical and mythical material. In Rabinal he unearthed the Quiche Bible, the *Popol Vuh*, a document of fundamental importance on the cosmology and religion of the Quiche people, one of the main branches of the Maya family. In San Juan Sacatapéquez he rescued from oblivion the *Memorial of Sololá*, written in the Cakchiquel language. As parish priest of Rabinal, responsible for a native population of seven thousand souls, he had no qualms—as he himself very engagingly explains—about persuading the Indians to perform for him the old ballet play *Rabinal Achi* so that he could take down the words and translate the play into French. He also found time to learn Nahuatl and Maya, visit the ruins in central and southern Mexico, write a monumental though not entirely reliable *History of the Civilised Nations of Mexico and Central America*, and translate and publish a great variety of documents. His last journey to Tehuantepec, Mexico and Guatemala in 1859–1860 was the only one on which he was charged with an official scientific mission, the Ministry of Education having at last thought fit to grant him this distinction.

Brasseur was, of course, still a long way short of our present-day conception of an archaeologist. Intoxicated by the fantastic wealth of material he discovered, he cast his net widely, taking an interest in whatever came his way. He was always ready—too ready—to find similarities, to seek parallels in the Old World or even in the lost continent of Atlantis, as the eccentric American explorer Le Plongeon was later to do also. But we must still pay tribute to him as the man who made available to scholars documents of priceless value like the *Popol Vuh,* and the pioneer who achieved recognition for American studies as a discipline no less respectable than classical archaeology.

This is an important contribution, for we must remember that in the second half of the 19th century American antiquities were still considered as no more than barbarous curios unworthy of the attention of an educated man. Brasseur protested vigorously in 1861 (preface to his edition of the *Popol Vuh*) against the attitude of the authorities of the Louvre: "American antiquities", he wrote, "which their inveterate detractors persist in regarding as mere barbarous toys, have been... transferred from the lower vestibule to the upper vestibule and then relegated to a dark corridor to await their next move... How little attention is paid to the fine vases from Guatemala and Peru, so much superior as examples of the art of pottery to the vases of Egypt and Etruria!... Why cannot funds be provided for an expedition to go to Uxmal, Palenque or Mitla, as it might go to the banks of the Euphrates or the Nile, in quest of the fine sculpture to be found there?"

Brasseur was among the first in France, if not the very first, to launch the idea of "pre-Columbian art" which is now in general use, and to claim that ancient Mexico and Peru were no less worthy of investigation than Egypt and Mesopotamia. He managed to secure the interest of influential men like Mérimée and Renan, of the Académie des Inscriptions et Belles-Lettres, and of the French government itself.

He was not the only one to enter this still unexplored field. The name of J.M.A. Aubin deserves to be specially remembered, for he was instrumental in rescuing an extraordinary quantity of material from neglect and destruction. Born in 1802, Aubin took part in the French revolution of July 1830, and in the same year set off for Mexico to carry out physical and astronomical observations. He soon became passionately interested in the native civilisations, visiting the sites and studying the ruins. In private and public collections in Mexico he was able to see nearly four thousand objects—pieces of sculpture, idols, urns, etc.—which, he wrote, "belied the generally accepted view of native art as completely stationary." Most important of all, he became acquainted with the life and work of Boturini.

The Cavaliere Lorenzo Boturini Benaduci, Baron de la Torre y Hono, a scion of a noble Milanese family who also traced his descent from the ruling family of Aquitaine and other French families of high rank, was born in Sondrio in 1702. He arrived in Mexico in 1376 as the authorised representative of the Countess of Santibáñez, Manuela de Oca Silva y Motecuhzuma, commissioned to recover funds in New Spain belonging to his noble employer and to secure the payment to her of a pension of a thousand piastres a year which was due to her as a descendant of the Imperial Aztec dynasty. A man of intense curiosity and unusual energy, Boturini fell in love with Mexico and its past. Within seven years he managed to assemble a magnificent collection of original documents, illustrated and pictographic manuscripts, ancient maps and plans, and texts in Aztec and in Latin characters. Unfortunately the authorities of Spanish America, civil and religious, were highly suspicious of his activities. He was a foreigner; he concerned himself with religious subjects (he thought, for example, of writing a *History of the Apparition of Our Lady of Guadalupe*); and he seemed also to have designs on the public purse. In February 1743, therefore, he was arrested, thrown into prison, and stripped of all his property, including his precious collection. After eight months in prison he was unceremoniously expelled from the country by being put forcibly aboard a ship sailing from Veracruz for Spain.

His tribulations, however, were not yet over; for the ship was captured by British privateers and he found himself once again in prison. Finally he was put ashore at Gibraltar with nothing to his name but two piastres and the sailor's outfit he wore, and from there found his way to Seville. King Philip V, recognising the value of his work and the injustice of the suspicions to which he had been exposed, appointed him Historiographer of the Indies with an annual salary of a thousand piastres, and ordered that all the documents which had been confiscated should be restored to him.

Boturini now remained in Spain and published his *Idea of a New General History of Northern America, based on a Considerable Collection of Figures, Symbols, Characters and Hieroglyphs, Hymns, and Manuscripts by Indian Authors* (1746). By the time of his death in 1749, however, the restitution ordered by the King had not taken place.

After Boturini's death his priceless collection suffered heavy loss. "It was removed", wrote the Mexican archaeologist Alfredo Chavero, "from the Viceroy's office to the University Library, from there to the Ministry of Foreign Affairs, and from there to the National Museum; and at each move it lost something." It lost so much that by the time Aubin arrived in Mexico most of the manuscripts and hieroglyphic texts had been dispersed. Aubin at once set about tracking down and recovering the lost documents, devoting to this task ten years of his life and the whole of the income he derived from the institute of secondary education which he had founded and continued to run. In 1840 he was able to return to France with the bulk of Boturini's collection.

In 1889 Aubin was compelled to sell the collection to Eugène Goupil, a wealthy and intelligent collector, who had been born in Mexico, the son of a French father and an Aztec mother; and Goupil in turn bequeathed the collection to the Bibliothèque Nationale in Paris. The collection contains many items of extreme rarity (the *Codex Ixtlilxochitl*, the Aubin *Tonalamatl*, the *Mapa Quinatzin*, the *Codex of 1576*, the *Toltec-Chichimec Annals*, etc.), and is one of the main sources of our knowledge of the ancient native civilisations of Mexico. A magnificent and erudite *catalogue raisonné* of the collection, with a volume of reproductions, was published in 1891 by Eugène Boban.

In Paris Aubin naturally came into contact with Brasseur de Bourbourg and a whole galaxy of scholars interested in American antiquity. Among these were Rémi Siméon, a former pupil of Aubin's in his school in Mexico City and the author of an Aztec grammar and a translation of the *Annals* of Chimalpahin; Léon de Rosny, who attempted to decipher the Maya script; the linguist Charles de Charencey, the great geographer Malte-Brun, Jomard, Cortambert and Ernest Renan. The Société Américaine de France was founded in Paris in 1863 for the study of the peoples, the languages and the civilisations of the New World, counting among its founder members Aubin, Rosny, the colourful "Count" de Waldeck, Emile Burnouf, Alphonse Pinart (who was to bring back to France an important collection of Mexican antiquities), Brasseur de Bourbourg, a Prince Bibesco, and scholars from Belgium, Germany, Russia, Switzerland, Spain and South America. The first International Congress of Americanists was held in Nancy on 19th July 1875, establishing a tradition which, in spite of two world wars, has been maintained to the present day; and the International Congress has continued to meet, usually every four years, in Europe and America alternately.

Archaeology and Pre-Columbian Art

As can be gathered from this account, the French research effort in the field of Mexican antiquities had hitherto been concerned mainly with the study of written documents, involving epigraphists, philologists and linguists. With E.T. Hamy (1842–1908) the examination of the documents was reinforced by a systematic study of the material remains. Originally a prehistorian, Hamy took an interest in the long neglected collections of American antiquities which were transferred in 1878 from the Louvre; to the New Museum of Ethnography in the Trocadéro. He became Director of this Museum and lectured on the Indians of ancient America; in 1897 he published two magnificent volumes on the American Gallery in the Museum; and he discovered in the library of the Chambre des Députés one of the finest pre-Columbian manuscripts, the *Codex Borbonicus (Plate 175)*, of which he published an excellent reproduction accompanied by scholarly notes. A few years later Dr Louis Capitan, who had been a close associate of Eugène Boban's while he was working on the Boturini-Aubin collection, became a convert to American studies, and travelled and studied in Mexico; and in 1908 he was appointed to the Chair of American Antiquities founded by the Duc de Loubat at the Collège de France, which he continued to occupy until his death in 1929[3].

It would be wrong to omit the Duc de Loubat's name from this account; for this wealthy patron was responsible for the publication of Hamy's works and of several Codices, the foundation of Capitan's Chair in Paris and Eduard Seler's in Berlin, and the acquisition by the Trocadéro Museum of many casts of Mexican monuments and carvings. This enlightened and generous *grand seigneur* belonged to a species which now seems to be as totally extinct as the mammoth of Tepexpán.

[3] The Fondation Loubat having been impoverished by the devaluation of the franc, the Chair of American Antiquities was replaced, up to the 1939–45 war, by a lectureship, which the author of this work had the honour of holding in 1938–39.

Hamy and Capitan, with the Duc de Loubat, were among the founders of the Société des Américanistes, which succeeded the Société Américaine de France in 1895. This society is still in existence and still publishes its scholarly *Journal*, one of the world's leading scientific journals concerned with the ethnology and archaeology of the New World. Its leading spirit from 1922 to 1958 was Dr Paul Rivet who, as Director of the Museum of Ethnography and later of the Musée de l'Homme, Professor at the National Museum of Natural History and founder of the Institute of Ethnology, devoted the major part of his energies to South America but still found time to concern himself with Mexico. His researches on the Indians of Lower California and on the working of gold and bronze, his magnificent publication on the Maya cities, and his volume of photographs of Mexican pre-Columbian art all demonstrate the interest which this outstanding pioneer in the study of man took in the peoples and cultures of Mexico.

The study of Mexican archaeology in France received a powerful stimulus with the establishment of the Trocadéro Museum (1878), which in 1937 became the Musée de l'Homme. The collections—in particular the Angrand and Latour-Allard collections—in which the Louvre had shown so little interest, and which E.T. Hamy had saved from destruction during the siege of Paris in 1871, at last found a fitting home here; and the Museum became the central point for the archaeologists and travellers who were now bringing back material and photographs. Désiré Charnay, an intrepid explorer and a first class photographer, paid two visits to Mexico and Yucatán (1857–1860, 1880–1884), discovered the sculpture of Yaxchilán, brought back excellent casts of carvings, and made contact with the Lacandone Indians. Although his theories have now been superseded, he is entitled to the merit of having drawn the attention of scholars to the similarities between the architecture and sculpture of the Toltecs on the central plateau and the corresponding arts in Yucatán. His books, *Cités et ruines américaines* (1863, in collaboration with Viollet-le-Duc) and *Les anciennes villes du Nouveau-Monde* (1885), are still worth reading. Auguste Genin,

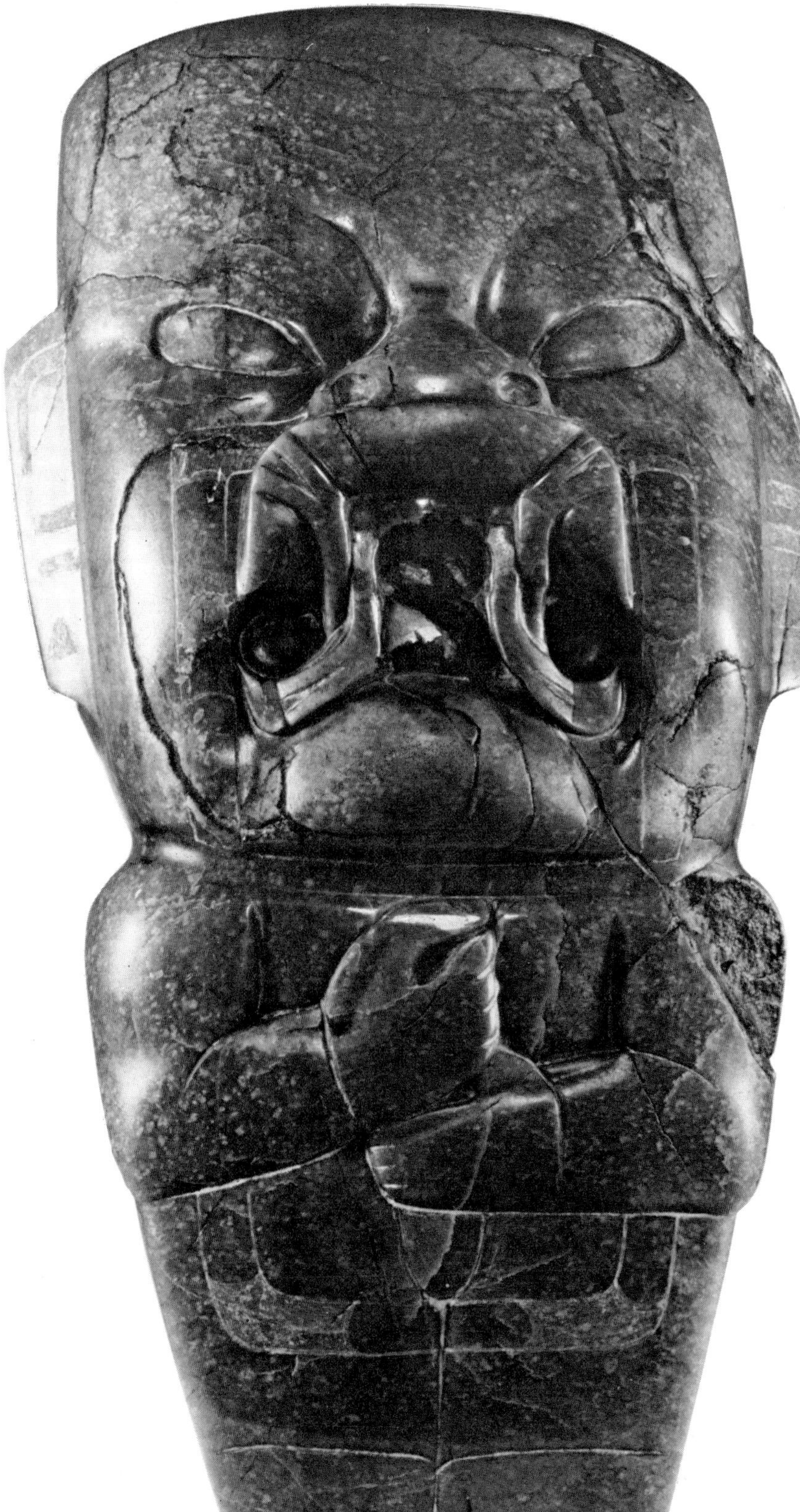

28

29

30

31

32

34, 35→

33

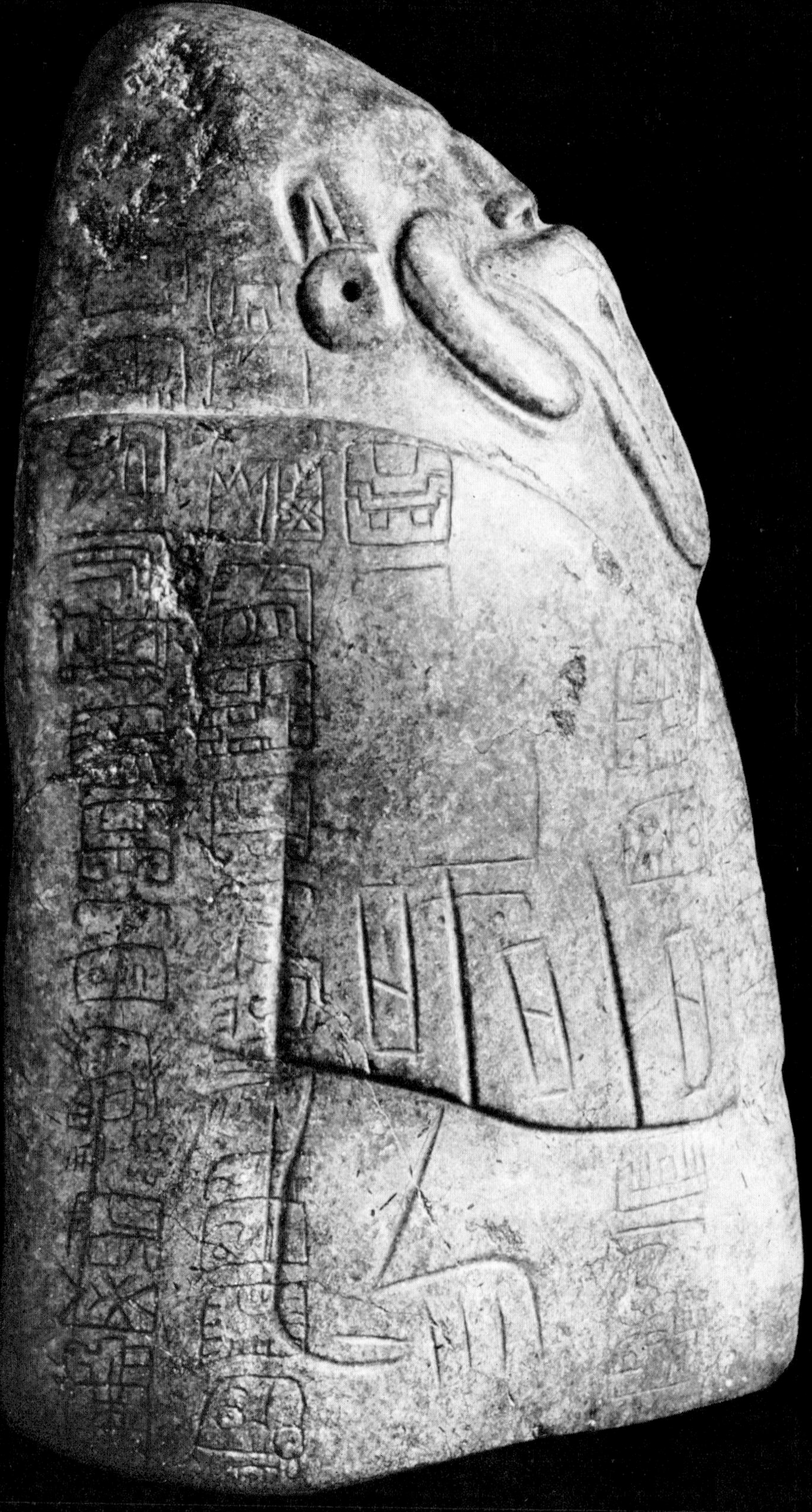

41 →

37

38

39

40

42

43

44

45

46

47

48, 49→

50

51

52

53

54→

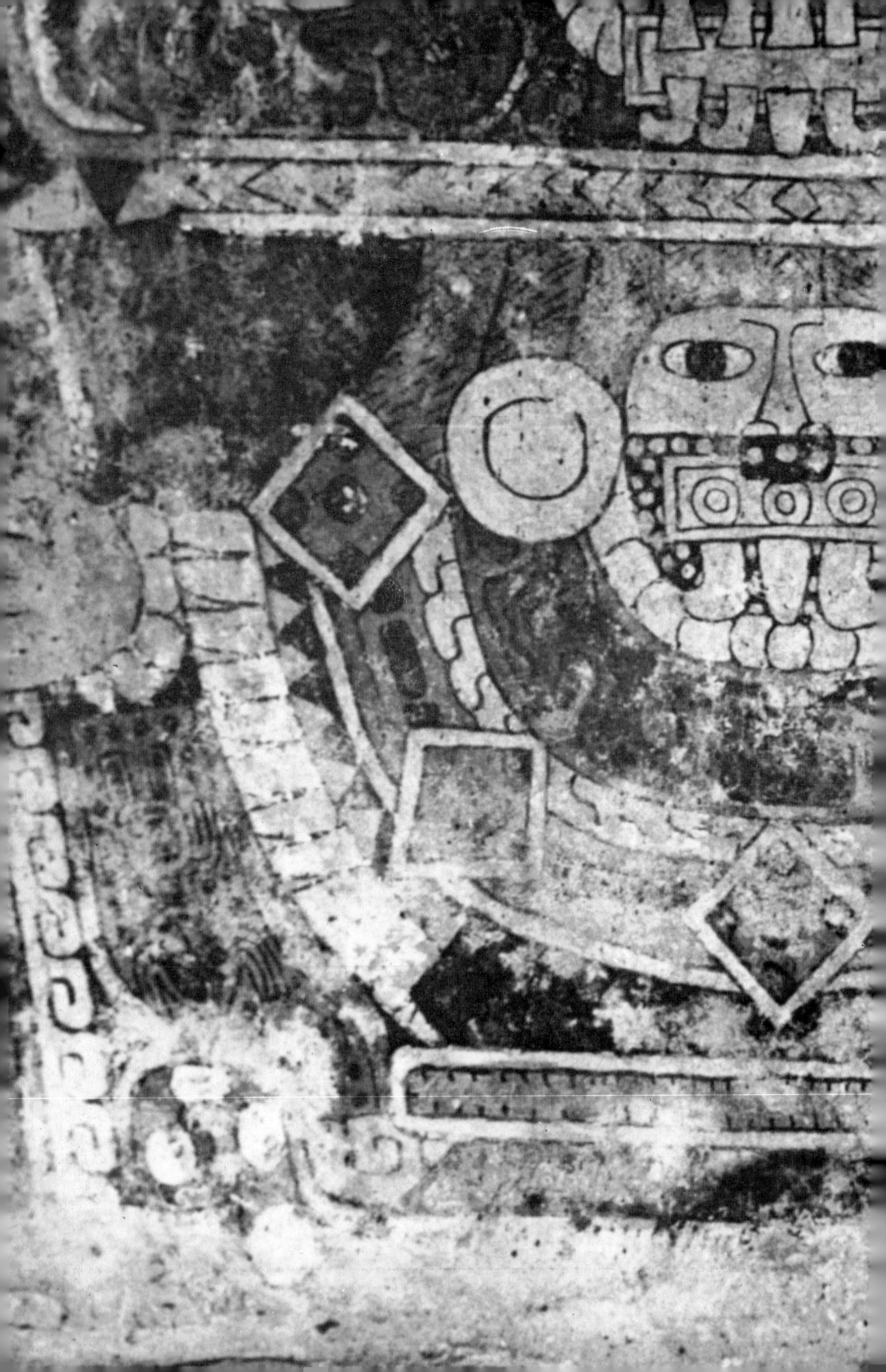

55

who was born in Mexico but spent some years in Paris towards the end of the century, was one of the select group of enthusiastic students of Mexican antiquity who gathered round Eugène Boban; returning to Mexico, he amassed a considerable collection of material which found a home in the Trocadéro Museum. The Museum also received a bequest from Alphonse Pinart of a collection of over 3000 vases, statues and carvings, including the famous Aztec skull in rock crystal, the only piece comparable to which is in the British Museum.

As research increasingly moved from the library to the field, from philology to archaeology in the proper sense of the term, from the study of documents to the study of the material remains, the intellectual world of Europe and North America became steadily more aware of what is now called pre-Columbian art. But it took many years to outlive the state of mind which applied the epithet "primitive" or even "savage" to pieces of ancient Mexican sculpture or pottery which were often authentic masterpieces. It is astonishing to read, for example, the remarks by Stoebel, Keeper of the St Petersburg Museum, at the first International Congress in Nancy in 1875:

"From the aesthetic and artistic point of view," he declared categorically, "no ancient civilisation has so little to show as that of America... This absence of any plastic beauty in native American art may not concern ethnographers and archaeologists, but artists must deplore it, and it is a fact of supreme importance to the historian; for he may deduce from it that the ancient Americans, being without any feeling for beauty, were also without any moral sense."

It can be seen from this that Brasseur de Bourbourg, the modest parish priest, had a clearer understanding of Mexican art than the Russian "specialist".

In 1928 the French public was given its first opportunity to see and admire pre-Columbian art. The exhibition of "The Ancient Arts of America" organised in the Pavillon de Marsan in Paris by Georges-Henri Rivière and Alfred Métraux was an important landmark: henceforth it was generally recognised that the native inhabitants of America had created works of art which, strange or displeasing as they might be to a taste formed by the European tradition, were nevertheless worthy of being included in the common heritage of mankind. From now on archaeology, though still concerned with the humblest scraps of domestic pottery and with simple undecorated tombs, was always to comprehend an interest in the study and the history of art.

Recent Exploration and Excavation

The last decades of the 19th century were marked by the explorations of the British archaeologist A.P. Maudslay (1881–1894); the results of his study of the ruined Maya cities were published in five splendid volumes illustrated with photographs and drawings of exemplary accuracy. The German Teobert Maler travelled widely in the empty region of Petén and in the interior of Yucatán, sending a series of reports, illustrated with excellent photographs, to the Peabody Museum at Harvard.

In the closing years of the 19th and the early years of the 20th century Mexico itself awoke to the realisation of its splendid past. Outstanding scholars like Joaquín García Icazbalceta, Francisco Pimentel, Nicolás León and Manuel Orozco y Berra, and archaeologists like Chavero and Leopoldo Batres prepared the way for the modern generation, including men like Manuel Gamio, Pablo Martínez del Río, Alfonso Caso, Ignacio Marquina, Alberto Ruz L'Huillier, Miguel Covarrubias, Eduardo Noguera, Ignacio Bernal and many others, who combine immense energy and enthusiasm with exact and scientific excavation techniques, a rigorous classification of the material, and an ever more thorough study of the sources.

The first excavations at Teotihuacán, for example, were undertaken by Leopoldo Batres in 1905 and were concerned with the Pyramid of the Sun, *(Plate 41)*, the Temple of Quetzalcoatl or "Citadel", and the Temple of Agriculture. Batres was criticised for his rough and ready excavation methods—with some justification, for he brought about the collapse of part of the Pyramid of the Sun; but it is fair to say that at this period the technique of excavation was still at a fairly rudimentary stage. Later, after an interruption due to the civil war, the methodical exploration of the huge ancient city was resumed—by Gamio in 1917 and then by a number of Mexican and European archaeologists, including the Swede Sigvald Linné. The Mexican archaeologist Ignacio Bernal estimates that it will take at least half a century to complete the exploration of this site. And all the time fresh discoveries are being made, rewarding the efforts of the archaeologists but at the same time raising new problems: a recent example is the discovery in 1962 of the "Palace of Quetzalpapalotl".

Elsewhere on the central plateau, in the Valley of Mexico, systematic excavation has taken the history of the Mexican people back to a remote past, bringing to light traces of the cultures which were long called "archaic" and remains of one of the prehistoric inhabitants of Mexico, "Tepexpán Man", who hunted the mammoth 15,000 years before our era.

In the Oaxaca valley the ruins of Mitla and Monte Albán, with their frescoed tombs and their marvellous gold jewellery, were excavated by Mexican archaeologists under the leadership of Alfonso Caso; and as a result of this work we can now follow the development of the civilisations of the Zapotecs and the Mixtecs over a period of nearly two thousand years *(Plates 88, 90–100, 136)*.

On the Gulf Coast practically nothing has been done. It is scarcely more than twenty years since Matthew Stirling published the results of his explorations and excavations, which revealed the existence of the refined art of the Olmec civilisation. The great classic city of El Tajín *(Plates 108, 109)*, which was studied by José García Payón, has not yielded a hundredth part of its treasures: here too there is material for half a century of continuous effort. Farther north, little is known of Huaxtec archaeology, now the subject of study by a French expedition led by Guy Stresser-Péan.

A whole galaxy of American scholars have concentrated on Maya territory, and have some considerable achievements to their credit. Supported by museums and scientific institutions like the Peabody Museum, the Carnegie Institution and the Pennsylvania University Museum, archaeologists like Sylvanus G. Morley, Linton Satterthwaite, Tatiana Proskouriakoff, Edwin M. Shook and J. Eric S. Thompson have done valuable work in Yucatán and Petén, at Chichén Itzá, Uaxactún, Tikal, Piedras Negras and elsewhere. At Palenque Alberto Ruz L'Huillier, of the Mexican Institute of Anthropology and History, made one of the most striking discoveries of recent years, the crypt of the Temple of the Inscriptions *(Plates 62, 65, 66)*.

In parallel with these field excavations, research has continued into the written documents and inscriptions, calendric systems and methods of divination, and the symbolism of Mexican art. In this field the outstanding name is that of the great German Mexicanist Eduard Seler, whose work shows inexhaustible learning and a profound knowledge of the languages, myths and social organisation of the ancient Mexicans. The excellent works by Walter Krickeberg on the Totonacs and on the ancient civilisations of Mexico are based on Seler's methods.

The archaeology of Mexico can be divided into three phases—first the phase of direct observation in the 16th century; then the quest for written documents and the exploration of the sites; and finally the phase of systematic study. But it need hardly be said that this tidy classification, like other classifications, does not entirely fit the facts. Dupaix and Stephens, for example, went beyond mere exploration; and on the other hand we are still a long way from finding and listing all the documents or identifying all the sites.

Indeed, what strikes us most when we try to assess the present state of Mexican archaeology is the number and scale of the problems still to be solved and—in spite of the great progress that has been made—the immense gaps in our knowledge which still remain to be filled.

THE PROBLEMS OF MEXICAN ARCHAEOLOGY

II

Problems of Geography

As we have seen, Mexican archaeology did not spring fully armed from the brain of a single scholar or a group of scholars. It can point to no sudden breakthrough like Champollion's reading of the Egyptian hieroglyphs, no sensational revelations like those of Sir Arthur Evans in Crete. It went through more than a century of groping and uncertainty before it was able to assert itself as an independent discipline, to become something more than a branch of philology, and to reach beyond the superficial examination of the accessible remains and the uninformed curiosity of enthusiastic amateurs. (We can hardly blame the amateurs for falling into error, however, at a time when the field was almost entirely unexplored).

Today Mexican archaeology, having outgrown the difficulties of its long and gradual development, is concerned with a whole series of intractable problems; and the first problems it faces are those created by the extent of territory with which it has to deal—for Mexico is a world in itself.

If we take the term Mexico, in the archaeological sense, to include the whole of the present country of Mexico together with the areas in Guatemala, Salvador, the Republic of Honduras and British Honduras in which the Maya civilisation attained its peak, we are concerned with a territory of more than three-quarters of a million square miles which is traversed by the Tropic of Cancer and belongs to both North and Central America. This is more than twice the size of ancient Egypt. Moreover this great area is subdivided into a large number of separate regions by its tormented geography and its wide variety of climate. The precipitous mountains and the high sierras, the great rivers, the swamps and the deserts break it up into compartments with widely varying physical and biological conditions—the steppes of the North with their cactuses, the enclosed valleys like the Valley of Mexico and the Oaxaca Valley, the hot humid forests of Chiapas and Petén, the high plateaux of central Mexico and Guatemala, the coastal regions on the Atlantic and Pacific. And as our knowledge increases we see that all these areas were inhabited by man at one period or another, in many cases through a number of successive phases.

It is a familiar fact that a man cannot dig a trench or cut the foundations of a house in the Valley of Mexico without coming across scraps of pottery, pieces of worked stone or javelin points; and the same thing is true of most parts of Mexico. Travelling through Mexico, or flying over certain parts of the country, we can discern under the mantle of vegetation the geometric shapes of earthworks and tumuli. In countless villages in Mexico we can see fragments of carved stone, built into the walls of churches or former religious houses, which have come from ancient sites in the neighbourhood.

It is convenient to classify the archaeological areas in four broad categories.

1. In some areas there have been systematic excavations over a long period, which have already produced valuable results. To this category belong the Valley of Mexico, particularly as regards the "archaic" sites (Copilco, Zacatenco, Ticomán, El Arbolillo, Tlatilco and Cuicuilco); the Teotihuacán and Tenayuca areas, near Mexico City; the Tula area in the state of Hidalgo; Cholula and Tizatlán, on the high plateau of Puebla-Tlaxcala; the Oaxaca valley, with the splendid sites of Monte Albán and Mitla; most of Yucatán (Chichén Itzá *(Plates 125, 126, 130, 131)*, Uxmal, Labná, Kabah, Sayil, Edzná, Mayapán, Tulum, etc.); Palenque in the state of Chiapas *(Plates 56–66);* Uaxactún, Tikal and Piedras Negras in Petén; Copán in Honduras; and a number of sites (Kaminaljuyú, Mixco Viejo) in the highlands of Guatemala. In these areas teams of experienced archaeologists with considerable resources at their disposal have devoted themselves—often over a long period of years—to clearing the ancient buildings, to establishing their structure and relationship to one another

and to studying the pottery, the sculpture and the wall paintings. And yet we are still a long way from being able to claim that our knowledge of these sites is complete.

In Mexico City there is the particular difficulty that the remains of the Aztec capital have been covered over, first by the town built by the Spaniards and then by the great modern city. As we have already noted, some important remains have been discovered in the course of building and civil engineering operations. Near the Cathedral, part of the old staircase of the *Great Teocalli*, with its balustrades decorated with serpents' heads, was brought to light. But the main part of the pre-Hispanic city of Tenochtitlán lies buried and inaccessible under the streets and buildings of the modern town.

2. In other areas numbers of ancient sites are known, some buildings have been excavated or protected against collapse, and provisional conclusions have been reached; but many years of work and heavy expenditure would be required to achieve further progress. Examples of this category are Xochicalco, on the western slope of the central plateau, where particular attention has been paid to the pyramid with its splendid carvings; El Tajín, near the Gulf Coast, where several hundred tumuli overgrown with dense vegetation surround the pyramid *(Plate 108)*, the palaces and the ball courts which have been excavated; many Maya sites, for example Yaxchilán; and La Venta, the Olmec centre in the state of Tabasco.

3. In some other areas the extent of our ignorance is still greater. The Huaxteca has yielded statues *(Plates 149–151)* and carvings, a very individual style of pottery and the Tamuín frescoes. The whole coastal area of Veracruz is covered with sites (possibly Olmec) of varying degrees of antiquity and some more recent (Totonac) sites, most of which have yielded an abundance of material, particularly pottery. On the opposite side of the central plateau, in the state of Michoacán, archaeological research has

barely begun. In the north are the remains of La Quemada, Chalchihuites and Casas Grandes; and in the state of Sinaloa excavations by Gordon F. Ekholm have revealed the fine pottery of Guasave.

The huge coastal mountainous area which occupies most of the states of Colima and Nayarit and part of Jalisco state has long yielded a wealth of terracotta objects—figurines, vases, and countless representations of men and animals—of outstanding artistic quality *(Plates 7, 8, 15–18, 21, 27)*. But most of these pieces have been taken from tombs without any scientific examination, so that their chronology is very difficult to establish.

4. Finally there are large areas, protected by distance and the nature of the terrain, which still remain blank on the archaeological map, though a few sites have been reconnoitred. This is the case, for example, in the large forest area of the Lacandones in the Chiapas country, where the fresco-covered walls of Bonampak were discovered in 1946 and certain other sites have been identified (Tzendales, Agua Escondida). The valleys of the Río Balsas and the Mezcala and the mountains of Guerrero and western Oaxaca have remained almost entirely unexplored, though we have figurines of hard stone from this area in a very characteristic style *(Plate 45)*. The Sierra Gorda, which forms a barrier between the states of Hidalgo, Querétaro and San Luis Potosí and is now almost uninhabited, was occupied in ancient times, as the remains of Toluquilla and Ranas testify; but practically nothing is known of these sites. The whole of this area is covered with mounds and other archaeological remains to which the Indians give the name of "Moctezuma", the last Aztec ruler.

Even if the necessary resources were available from either public or private sources—and this is very far from being the case—it would require several generations of archaeologists, with large numbers of trained assistants and a substantial labour force, to tackle the problems on a broad front and advance the bounds of our knowledge in all these areas. In spite of the splendid results achieved within the last twenty years by excavations like those of Alfonso Caso at Monte Albán, Ruz L'Huillier at Palenque and the Americans in Petén, the extent of our ignorance is incomparably greater than the area of our knowledge.

Problems of Chronology

Archaeological research thus faces problems created by the immense area and the very large number of sites with which it has to deal; but its difficulties also arise from the succession of civilisations which have followed one another on the same sites throughout the centuries. The time scale, with which archaeologists have necessarily had to concern themselves since the beginning of their work on Mexico, has steadily expanded as new finds and the systematic study of existing remains and excavated material have taken scholars ever farther back into the past.

The archaeological evidence on the peoples of Mexico available at the beginning of this century added up to a fairly simple and straightforward picture. The Aztecs and their contemporaries the Totonacs, the Zapotecs and other peoples, occupied the foreground; in the background was the great Toltec civilisation, to which were attributed even the pyramids of Teotihuacán. Following the scheme of things recorded by the native historians, the archaeologists agreed that the tribes of Mexico City, Texcoco, Azcapotzalco and other important places in the central valley had invaded the plateau in recent times, had found there the survivors and the material remains of the Toltec era, and had been refined by contact with their civilisation.

The more distant past was lost in the mist of legend. As always happens in these circumstances, some scholars sought to interpret the legends as a transposition of historical facts, while others subjected them to strict critical examination and found them to be mere fabulous tales concerned with the doings of gods rather than men. It was the achievement of Eduard Seler to unravel a large part of this tangled skein; and as a result of the work of Seler and his followers we can now see the myths of the civilised peoples of Mexico as reflecting simultaneously not only their cosmological and theological ideas but also certain historical events.

Thus, for example, Quetzalcoatl, the "Feathered Serpent", is on the one hand the civilising god, the inventor of writing and the arts, and the divinity of the Morning Star, and on the other the priest-king who was compelled to abandon Tula shortly before the year 1000 under pressure from warlike tribes; Tezcatlipoca *(Plates 157, 158, 169)*, the redoubtable sorcerer and god of the Great Bear, symbolises the warlike peoples who came down from the north and destroyed the theocratic structures of the classic period; and Xolotl *(Plates 155, 156)* is both a god—Quetzalcoatl's double and twin—who descended into the underworld and returned to the world of the living, and the leader of the "barbarian" tribes who occupied the central plateau after the fall of Tula and soon established a new civilisation based in essentials on that of the Toltecs.

Excavation has, however, thrown entirely fresh light on the succession of the native civilisations, and has shown that the picture is much more complex than had been thought.

At the end of last century the American archaeologist Zelia Nuttall realised the significance of certain objects—particularly terracotta figurines—which were given the label "archaic" and were found in great quantity in collections of material from the Valley of Mexico. In 1911–1912 Manuel Gamio discovered at San Miguel Amantla, near Azcapotzalco, pottery of "archaic" type buried under a layer of lava; and *above* the lava were remains belonging to the Teotihuacán civilisation. It was thus established that the "archaic" objects were earlier than the Teotihuacán period.

Excavations carried out in 1912 on the western shore of Lake Texcoco, now almost completely dried up, showed that Aztec remains appeared almost on the surface; under them, in a stratum 13 feet deep, were found objects of Teotihuacán type; and lower still was a stratum 5 feet deep containing "archaic" figurines.

The decisive discovery was made by Manuel Gamio in 1917, when he found an "archaic" cemetery in the Pedregal area, under a lava flow from the volcano of Xitle. There was no longer any room for doubt about the high antiquity of these remains. Thus the accepted picture of the history of ancient Mexico had to be substantially modified; for it was now clear that before the great cities like Teotihuacán there had been villages of farmers, hunters and fishermen who had tilled the soil, woven agave fibres, and moulded clay.

These Indian villagers had had on several occasions to abandon their villages, either under a rain of fire and ashes from the neighbouring volcanoes or because of flooding due to a rise in the level of the lake. The excavations of the American George C. Vaillant (1928–1932), the Norwegian Ola Apenes (1939) and the Mexican Miguel Covarrubias (1943 and following years) have thrown light on the successive phases of the "archaic" culture. It has been possible to subdivide it into two main forms, the Zacatenco and the Ticomán cultures. The tombs at Copilco belong to the former, while the Cuicuilco pyramid, half buried in a lava flow, dates from the most recent phase of the latter.

Zelia Nuttall suggested that the Aztec myths referring to the catastrophes which were supposed to have destroyed the world which existed before the present one (the myth of the Four Suns) reflected actual events; and this theory seems to find confirmation from a study of the sites of Zacatenco and Copilco, where there was a disastrous flood followed by a volcanic eruption which covered the villages with a lava flow some 25 feet deep.

Vaillant was able to subdivide the Zacatenco culture into two main phases and the Ticomán culture into three, taking as his criteria the types of vases and terracotta figurines. Moreover an examination of skeletons has shown that the transition between the two cultures was accompanied by a slight change in the physical type, indicating that a group of incomers had settled on the high plateau.

Radiocarbon dating enables us to assign the beginnings of maize agriculture in central Mexico and the oldest phase of the "archaic" styles to the 3rd millennium B.C. The eruption of Xitle is dated to shortly before the beginning of our era.

The discovery in 1947 at Tepexpán, near Mexico City, of human bones associated with skeletons of mammoths and stone weapons opened up a new prospect extending still farther back into the past; for Tepexpán Man must have lived fifteen or twenty thousand years before our era. He knew nothing of agriculture, but hunted the large animals which still lived at that period in the jungles and swamps, in a climate which seems to have been warmer and moister than it is today.

We are thus presented with a picture—still necessarily a provisional one—in which Tepexpán Man represents the real "archaic" culture, while the peoples of Zacatenco, Copilco and Ticomán, who were previously called archaic, can now be described as "pre-classic", or alternatively as belonging to the "middle cultures".

The pyramid of Cuicuilco, which can be dated from the lava flow which partly covers it to the end of the pre-classic period, is the first stone monument on the Mexican plateau. To be accurate, it is only partly built of stone, having a stone core, a main structure of sun-dried brick, and a stone facing. In the shape rather of a truncated cone than of a pyramid, the Cuicuilco monument has affinities with a whole range of structures of archaic type such as the oldest Maya pyramid at Uaxactún (E-VII-sub), the Huaxtec tumuli and the *yácatas* of Michoacán—all of which seem to have a common ancestor in the simple artificial earth mounds found in very large numbers all over the Mississippi and Ohio valleys. At Cuicuilco, however, the main features of the classic Mexican pyramids have already developed—the superimposed masses of masonry, with a staircase leading up to a terminal platform on which stood a sanctuary.

It is not, therefore, illogical to regard the final phase of Ticomán, to which Cuicuilco belongs, as marking the beginning of the transition to the great classic civilisations. This theory receives further support from a study of the magnificent tombs of Tlatilco, which belong to the same period; for in them we find not only an extraordinary abundance of the delicate figurines known as "fine ladies" *(Plates 2, 10–13)* but also, for the first time, the mark of the Olmec civilisation of the Gulf Coast.

The term "Olmec" is borrowed from the Aztec language, in which it was applied to the peoples of the Hot Lands on the shores of the Gulf. But we do not, of course, know who they were, what language they spoke, or where they came from, these men who created in the torrid jungles of Tabasco and Veracruz the earliest of the great Mexican civilisations. Here, before the beginning of our era, they developed the arts of architecture and sculpture, establishing ceremonial centres, building pyramids, erecting monolithic slabs of stone, carving bas-reliefs and devising a system of hieroglyphic writing which enabled them to record dates.

As early as the end of last century the Mexican archaeologist Alfredo Chavero had drawn attention to the Olmec remains in the Los Tuxtlas area. In 1925 Frans Blom and Oliver La Farge carried out a rapid reconnaissance of the area, but it was only in 1938 and the following years that Stirling, Weiant, Drucker and Covarrubias undertook the systematic excavation and study of the sites of La Venta, Tres Zapotes and Cerro de las

Mesas. And in spite of the astonishing abundance and extraordinarily high artistic quality of the material they discovered, this was probably a mere fraction of the treasure still lying hidden under the tropical jungles of the coastal area.

Olmec architecture is still fairly rudimentary, but the tumuli are faced with stone and are built in groups and sited on the cardinal points, as were all later Mexican monuments. The sculpture and carving achieve at once the highest artistic quality; and the advanced level of intellectual development which the Olmec civilisation had already reached is shown by its use of a script and an elaborate chronological system which anticipate the hieroglyphs and chronology of the Mayas.

Since—if we assume that the Maya system is comparable with that of the Olmecs—it is possible to read the dates inscribed on buildings or small objects, the Olmec civilisation can be dated between the 1st and the 6th centuries of our era (Stela of Tres Zapotes, 31 A.D.; Stela of Cerro de las Mesas, 593). It is not unreasonable to suppose that the Olmecs needed a "formative" period of two or three centuries to invent and to perfect their system of writing, their computation of time and their plastic arts *(Plates 28, 34, 35, 45)*. In its early stages, therefore, the Olmec civilisation would appear to have been contemporaneous with the terminal pre-classic phase on the central plateau.

This is confirmed by the discoveries at Tlatilco—in particular a splendid terracotta statuette of a child with typically Olmec features. Since the same characteristics are found at Monte Albán, in the bas-relief figures known as "Los Danzantes" and in certain pottery figurines, we can date the first two phases of the Zapotec civilisation of the Oaxaca *(Plates 90–93, 96–99)* valley to the beginning of our era, between 0 and 500. The pieces of the jigsaw thus fit together in a reasonably satisfactory way.

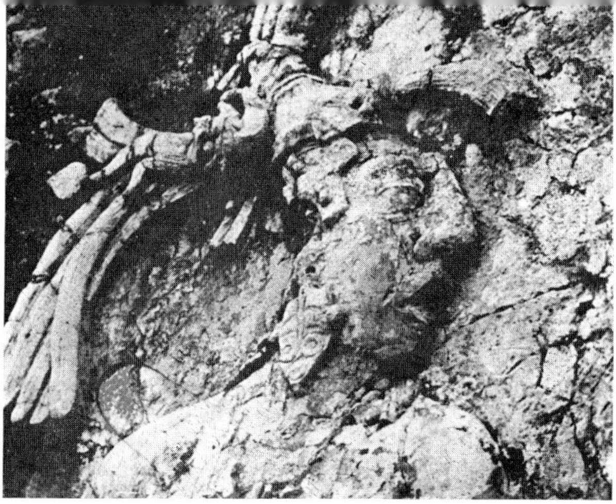

56

57

60 →

59

61

62

63

65, 66 →

64

68

69

71

72

73 →

Indeed we can go a stage farther for, as has been noted, the Olmec civilisation has certain features which we also find in the classic Maya civilisation—carved stelae, a system of hieroglyphs and a dating system. Now the oldest known Maya date (at Tikal) corresponds to the year 292 A.D., followed by the date of the Leyden Plate, a jade tablet in the Rijksmuseum in Leyden (320) *(Plates 67, 68)*, and the date on Stela 9 at Uaxactún (328). Thus if we postulate a "formative" period of two or three hundred years for the Mayas as well as for the Olmecs we can reasonably suppose that this period coincided with the flowering of the centres of Olmec culture.

Perhaps we may glimpse here the hint of an answer to the hitherto insoluble problem posed by the sudden appearance of the Maya civilisation in the 3rd century, already equipped with its characteristic attributes—its architecture, its sculpture, its hieroglyphic writing. May it not be that the Olmecs, whose influence extended so far beyond their area of settlement, into the central plateau and the mountains of Oaxaca, gave the Maya peoples of the tropical forests some of the fundamental ideas which they developed in such a remarkable fashion? In other words, must we not regard the Olmecs as a pre-Maya people? In order to throw more light on these problems we clearly need more excavation in Olmec territory. In the meantime we are perhaps doing no more than replacing the Maya enigma by an Olmec enigma; for in the present state of knowledge we have no clue to the origin of the Olmec civilisation or to the course of its development during its formative phase.

However this may be, we can see what a considerable change has come over our picture of the Mexican civilisations within the last few decades. From Palaeolithic man at Tepexpán to the successive Neolithic cultures of Zacatenco and Ticomán, from the Olmecs to the pre-classic peoples of the central plateau, the first inhabitants of Monte Albán and the Mayas, we see emerging a whole complex of facts and connections which were unknown a few years ago and have been revealed only as a result of unremitting effort by the excavators. The picture has been enlarged and become more complicated, the frontier between the known and the unknown has been pushed back three thousand years, and forgotten peoples, with their arts and their religions, have been recovered from oblivion. In contrast, the great theocratic civilisations of Teotihuacán, Monte Albán and the Maya territory are now seen as the expression of a classic period whose culmination varies between the 4th and the 7th centuries of our era in different areas; and the Toltecs, who were previously considered, following the Aztec tradition, as the source of all the advanced cultures of Mexico, are now seen to be merely skilled craftsmen belonging to a relatively recent period of revival. What used to be thought of as belonging to the most remote antiquity has now become a late phase of development.

And here archaeologists are confronted with a whole series of chronological problems. Did the final phase of the pre-classic cultures of Ticomán, Cuicuilco and Tlatilco precede the initial phase of Teotihuacán, or were these two phases contemporaneous? Did the Teotihuacán civilisation disappear and give place to the Toltec civilisation, or did the two civilisations co-exist for some time? How can we fit in the mythico-historical episode of the fall of Quetzalcoatl, his departure from Tula and the appearance of the "Feathered Serpent" at Chichén Itzá in Yucatán somewhere about the year 1000? We cannot answer questions like these with any real assurance. We can, in broad terms, distinguish a number of classic civilisations which developed round centres such as Teotihuacán on the plateau, El Tajín on the Gulf Coast, Monte Albán in Oaxaca, Tikal, Uaxactún, Palenque, Piedras Negras and Copán in the southern Maya territory, and Oxkintok, Uxmal, Tulum and Labná in Yucatán. We can date them—still very broadly—between 200 and 900 A.D.; but while Teotihuacán disappeared as a great cultural centre about the beginning of the 8th century the Maya cities continued to exist until the end of the 9th (the latest date in the Uaxactún carvings is 889), and Monte Albán, though in decline, lingered on until at a much later period it fell into the hands of the Mixtecs. Finally the period of revival began in 856 on the high plateau with the foundation of Tula and about the year 1000 in Yucatán (Chichén Itzá), and came to an end at roughly the same time in the north and the south, about the year 1200.

Until quite recently Maya archaeologists used the terms "Old Empire" and "New Empire" to designate the first (4th–9th centuries) and second (10th century to the Spanish conquest) phases of that civilisation: these expressions were still used, for example, by Sylvanus G. Morley, one of the leading authorities in this field, in his monumental work *The Ancient Maya*, published in 1946 (3rd edition, 1956). This terminology was associated with the generally accepted idea that the only, or almost the only, active cultural centres during the Old Empire were the southern Maya cities, in Chiapas, Guatemala and Honduras, and that in the New Empire the centres of civilised life moved to Yucatán. This classification has now been abandoned, for it has been realised that the peninsula of Yucatán was the scene of a brilliant and individual cultural development during the earlier phase, and it has become clear also that the term "Empire" cannot properly be applied to the Maya city states. What is established is that the towns of the south were abandoned one after the other by the priestly élite, and that the Toltec-Maya revival in Yucatán was impregnated with non-Maya influence from the Mexican high plateau.

And finally we know that the three centuries before the Conquest were marked, both in Maya territory and in central Mexico and Oaxaca, by extensive migrations, fierce struggles for predominance, the rise of militarism and the increasing importance of sacrificial rites. But whereas in Yucatán the endemic civil wars and the introduction of Mexican mercenaries led to a profound cultural decadence, in Oaxaca the Mixtecs showed that they possessed remarkable artistic and intellectual qualities, and the Aztecs—in spite of the excesses of their bloody ritual—built up a vigorous civilisation based on the Toltec tradition. In any event the liquidation of the great theocratic civilisations of the classic period had been completed before the discovery of America by the Europeans.

But while these urban civilisations, from the Olmecs to the Aztecs, were establishing themselves, developing, and then falling into decay, the whole of north-western Mexico (Colima, Nayarit, Jalisco) seems to have remained at the village stage of development. In this area we find a striking contrast between the wealth of pottery found in the tombs *(Plates 7, 16, 18, 21, 25–27)* and the complete absence of buildings, stelae or bas-reliefs. Certain terracotta objects, full of lively realism and humour, show us that these north-western farmers lived in simple houses of timber and thatch. Thus both their way of life and their art seem to represent a continuation of the pre-classic cultures. In the present state of knowledge, however, and in the absence of any systematic excavation, we cannot determine the course of development of this north-western culture—though it seems altogether unlikely that it remained stagnant and unchanging for two thousand years.

Writing and Chronology

A civilisation which invented a system of writing, and was so obsessed with the importance of chronology that it used its script to record exact dates, is evidently a special boon for archaeologists. In this respect the classic Maya civilisation is unique in the world, for no other known civilisation devoted so much effort to engraving, carving or painting hieroglyphs, the overwhelming majority of which are concerned with the recording of dates, the duration of the year and longer periods of time, the phases of the moon, the revolutions of Venus, the occurrence of eclipses, and so on. In spite of this, however, we are still a long way from solving all the problems raised by Maya writing and chronology.

Maya writing is found in two forms. There are, in the first place, the inscriptions carved in low relief on monuments or engraved on small objects like the Leyden Plate *(Plates 67, 68)*, made up of complex hieroglyphs of remarkable decorative effect, arranged in columns or in blocks, often in the blank spaces between figures in a carving. Each character consists of a cartouche, rectangular in shape with rounded corners, within which are signs known as "infixes", and is accompanied by a number of "affixes", usually below or to the right of the cartouche. The figures—which are of frequent occurrence, since most of the inscriptions are concerned with chronology and astronomy—are usually to the left of the cartouche. But there was also a form of "cursive" writing, to be seen in the three Maya manuscripts[4] which have survived the ravages of time and the fanaticism of man. These manuscripts are known to be copies of relatively recent date, but hieroglyphs of the same type are found on the walls of a tomb under the acropolis at Tikal which is dated to 457. Similar inscriptions are also found on ancient Guatemalan pottery and in wall paintings at Bonampak. In this script the forms of the characters are simplified, and they have lost all traces of naturalism and become purely abstract; but there is as a rule no difficulty in relating the two systems.

We must note, however, that the hieroglyphs used in the inscriptions occur in varying forms, showing different degrees of complexity and naturalism. The figures, for example, are represented by bars (for the figure 5) and dots (for the units) or by faces; in the latter case the faces of different gods are associated with particular numbers, which can be identified by the details of their hair style or tattooing. Zero may be represented by a stylised shell, a hand, or a symbol like a Maltese cross. Finally in some

[4] The *Codex Dresdensis* was discovered in 1739 in Vienna, where it had probably been brought along with other Mexican antiquities belonging to Charles V. It was later presented to the Royal Library of Dresden, and was published by Förstemann in 1880. The *Codex Tro-Cortesianus* was found in Spain, in two sections, during the 19th century. It is now in the Museum of Archaeology and History in Madrid. The *Codex Peresianus* turned up in the Bibliothèque Nationale in Paris in 1860; it was found in a hamper of old papers standing forgotten beside a fireplace. It was published by Léon de Rosny in 1887.

inscriptions, particularly at Palenque and Copán, we find hieroglyphs with tfull length figures, in which the numbers take on the form of living creaures and each cartouche contains an exquisitely delicate little picture.

A hieroglyphic script composed of characters enclosed in cartouches and figures represented by bars and dots is characteristic of all the advanced civilisations of Mexico. We find it as early as the Olmec period, for example in the Tuxtla Statuette *(Plate 34)*; and it is used by the Zapotecs of Monte Albán and—rarely—at Teotihuacán. Similar characters are found on the walls of the pyramid of Xochicalco, created by a civilisation which seems to have been a connecting link between Oaxaca, Teotihuacán and Tula. This system of writing must, therefore, have developed from a common source, though we are at present unable to identify this. It is possible that the script was devised, along with the calendar, somewhere on the western side of Mexico or in Petén by a pre-Olmec and pre-Maya people, who then passed it on to the civilisations of La Venta, Tikal and Monte Albán. At any rate this script is quite distinct in character from the script used at a later date by the Mixtecs and Aztecs. In this latter script the signs are much more realistic, each symbol clearly representing a particular object, animal or god (a house, a rabbit, the wind god, the rain god); the signs are not enclosed in cartouches; and the bar is no longer used to represent the figure 5, nor is there any symbol for zero. The Maya could write any number very simply in their vigesimal system, using figures with positional value and the symbol for zero as we do in our decimal system. Thus four hundred, which we write 400 (i.e., 0 units, 0 tens and 4 units of the third degree), became in the Maya system 1.0.0. (i.e., 0 units, 0 twenties and 1 unit of the third degree). In the Mixtec-Aztec scripts, as in the system used by the Romans, special symbols were used—dots for the units and other signs for twenty, four hundred and eight thousand. In this respect, therefore, the later civilisations were clearly far behind the civilisations of the classic period.

The Maya system of writing immediately raised two problems—the decipherment of the symbols themselves and the correlations between Maya dates and our own. Unfortunately neither problem has yet been completely solved.

Diego de Landa's *Account of the Affairs of Yucatán* contains a chapter which raised high hopes in the minds of many people, who saw in it the Rosetta Stone of the Maya hieroglyphs. In writing his *Account* the Bishop of Mérida had sought to reproduce certain hieroglyphs in a phonetic transcription. It has since been realised, however, that the Maya script was essentially ideographic, like the Chinese system of writing, even though certain signs—as in Egyptian—also served to denote a sound with a quite different meaning from the symbol itself. Thus, for example, the glyph *xoc* represents a certain kind of fish, but is also used to write the sound *xoc*—i.e., the verb and noun meaning "count". The symbol for the moon, *u*, likewise corresponds to the third person possessive, which is also pronounced *u*. Since the Maya language was rich in syllables with the same sound, and made little distinction between the substantive and the verb, its script could readily represent ideas and sounds which at the same time suggested other ideas or actions.

It seems to be established that the Mayas used the "rebus" method in the same way as did the Aztecs at a later period. Glyphs like *tun*, "stone", are used to form compound words like *katun*, *baktun*, etc.; *kin*, "sun", is found in *kankin*, *yaxkin;* and so on. Associations of ideas determined by religious and mythological tradition allowed the Maya reader to give each glyph the sense appropriate to the subject matter—to know, for example, whether the word *tun* was to be interpreted as meaning a stone, a piece of jade, a year, or as the indication of the end of a particular chronological period. The difficulty is that we know practically nothing of these associations of ideas, which we must laboriously piece together from the 16th century descriptions and chronicles, imperfect and late as they are.

There have been some ambitious attempts at decipherment based on Landa's supposed alphabet—for example, by the German Werner Wolff and the Russian Knorozov—but these have produced unconvincing results. More fruitful, though extremely slow and difficult—and more limited in scope—have been the researches of a large number of German, Mexican and American scholars like Förstemann, Hermann Beyer, P. Schellhas, Eduard Seler, Martínez Hernández, Barrera Vásquez, Bowditch, Goodman, J.E. Teeple, W. Gates, H.J. Spinden, Sylvanus G. Morley and J. Eric S. Thompson. Their work has been based on the internal study of the texts, on comparisons between different signs and different inscriptions, on the interpretation of each symbol or group of symbols with the help of all the available knowledge about the intellectual background and the beliefs of the ancient Mayas. Progress is slow, painful and tentative, proceeding from the known to the unknown; but as a result it has been possible to decipher dates, inscriptions relating to corrections of the calendar, the phases of the moon and the movements of the planet Venus, the signs indicating certain actions, or ideas like "good", "bad", "death", "drought", "rain" or "maize", and certain symbols with a phonetic value, like those mentioned above and others such as *yax*, *te*, *il*, *ak*, etc.

These studies lead to a surprising conclusion, disclosing that the great bulk of the inscriptions and manuscript texts refer to chronological and astronomical calculations. There are no historical records or eulogies of war leaders and kings, as in Egypt; no legislative texts, as in Babylon; no tablets recording trading accounts or tax lists, as in Asia Minor and Crete. All the texts we can decipher—about a third of those known—constitute a kind of hymn to eternity, an astonishing collection of calculations covering immense periods of time (400 million years at Quiriguá), a concentrated mass of dates, astronomical references, forecasts of eclipses, and portents for the future based on observations of heavenly bodies.

Must we conclude that the Maya inscriptions contained nothing more than this? Is it possible that the priests who evidently dominated the intel-

←74, 75, 76

79, 80

81

–77, 78

82

←83, 84

85

86

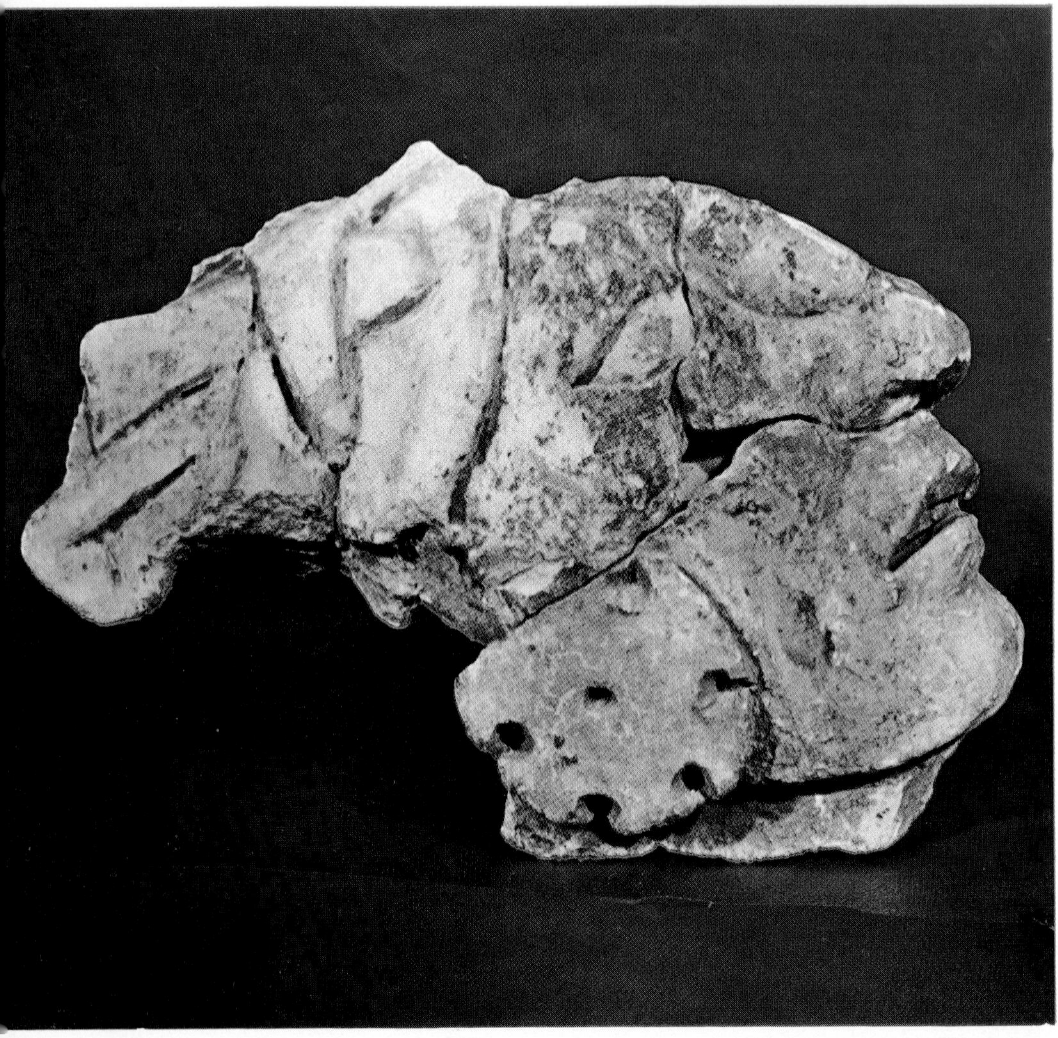

88, 89→

87

90

91

92

93

94 95

98, 99→

96

97

1

lectual and social life of this civilisation—their eyes turned perpetually skyward and their thoughts exclusively concerned with the measured passage of time—disdained to record the important events of their own history, as every other people has done and as the Aztecs in their day were also to do? Although many scholars, including in particular Thompson, are inclined to this view, it seems premature to reach such a conclusion. Tatiana Proskouriakoff has noted that the dates on the stelae of Piedras Negras, with their carved figures, might well correspond to the dates of birth or succession of kings or great lords. No doubt there were also signs—as at Monte Albán and, at a later period, at Mexico City—denoting the names of particular tribes or individuals. One of the warriors depicted in the Bonampak frescoes bears a hieroglyph which must denote his name or function. In a bas-relief at Piedras Negras there are some figures of captives of non-Maya type lying garrotted at the feet of a dignitary, with hieroglyphs on their body which probably represent the name of their tribe or their country. The magnificent carving at Palenque, the *Tablero de los Esclavos*, also seems to represent a historical event. The upper part shows a dignitary receiving sumptuous gifts from two suppliants or ambassadors, and below this is a long inscription containing 262 hieroglyphs. It is difficult to avoid the conclusion that this inscription records some historical event (perhaps the submission of a town, a treaty or an alliance) the concluding scene of which is shown in the upper part of the carving.

Nevertheless it is clear that most of the texts—and certainly those that have been deciphered so far—are concerned with astronomy and chronology. The chronological system which they reflect is one of astonishing complexity and precision. With its aid the Mayas of the classic period were able to fix a date without any possibility of error or ambiguity, determined the length of the year by an approximation which was more accurate than our Gregorian system, and could calculate the phase of the moon for any past or future date. They could also compute the movements of Venus with an error of less than two hours in five hundred years.

Since the Maya calendar is based on the same principles as the calendars used by all the civilised peoples of Mexico, from the Olmecs to the Aztecs, it may be worth while to summarise briefly its main features.

Any given date or day *(kin)* was designated by reference to two quite distinct calendars—a divinatory and ritual calendar of 260 days *(Plate 139)* in which each day had a number (from 1 to 13) and a name taken from a series of twenty, and a solar calendar of 365 days divided into 18 months of 20 days each, plus five unlucky days, the *uayeb*. The days of each month were numbered from 0 to 19. Thus the expression "8 *ahau* 13 *ceh*" meant the day which was numbered 8 in the series from 1 to 13, with the 20th name, and was the 14th day of the 12th month.

A simple calculation shows that a complete date with its four elements, fixing the position of a given day both in the ritual calendar of 260 days (Maya *tzolkin*, Aztec *tonalpohualli*) and in the solar calendar of 365 days (Maya *haab*, Aztec *xiuitl*), would recur in identical form only after 18,890 days—i.e., 73 *tzolkin* or 52 years.

The later civilisations of Mexico were content with this cycle of 52 years, which the Aztecs called the "year bundle", celebrating at the end of it the rite of the New Fire. The Mayas, however, were concerned to fix each date without any possibility of ambiguity; and throughout the classic period they achieved this by determining and recording in their inscriptions the exact number of days, months *(uinal)*, years *(tun)*, periods of twenty years *(katun)* and periods of four hundred years *(baktun)*[5] which had elapsed since a starting date in the year 3113 B.C. The chronological inscriptions thus consisted of what is known as an "Initial Series" made up

[5] The word "year" is used, but in fact the *tun* had only 360 days, so that the longer periods were actually slightly less than 20 and 400 years. A series of glyphs after the date made the necessary correction.

of a special hieroglyph introducing the series and five figures giving the number of periods which had elapsed since the starting date. If, for example, we take an inscription which is transcribed "8.15.10.0.0, 4 *ahau* 18 *pax*", this means that from the starting date to the day in question there had elapsed eight periods of four hundred years, fifteen periods of twenty years, and ten years exactly, with no additional months or days.

But the Mayas did not limit their vision of time to the period since 3113 B.C. This starting date was written "13.0.0.0.0"—i.e., they regarded it as the end of an earlier period which had lasted some 5000 years. In addition they used in their calculations, for both past and future dates, multiples of the *baktun* up to the period known as *alautun*, representing 23,040 million days, or some 63 million years. They had thus attained at a very early period a vision of the eternity of time—something which had neither beginning or end, but unfolded majestically and mysteriously through cycles which were continually renewed. And they had, too, invented zero and positional arithmetic, as the Greeks and Romans never did, more than a thousand years before the Indians made these discoveries, later to be handed on to Europe by the Arabs.

It is not possible to go into further detail here about other subjects treated in the ancient Maya texts. We may note, however, that the priestly astronomers had observed the apparent revolution of Venus, which lasts 584 days, and calculated that 65 Venusian years, or 37,960 days, were equivalent to 104 terrestrial years—i.e., to two of the 52-year cycles mentioned above. This discovery was preserved in priestly colleges throughout Mexico and was known to the Aztecs in the 15th century. The Dresden Codex contains Venusian and lunar tables of astonishing accuracy. It must have taken the Mayas several centuries to collect the observations on which these results were based, and this "formative" period must have begun in the early years of our era, or perhaps even before then.

Since the Mayas of the classic period were in the habit of dating their monuments, and also of erecting stelae at regular intervals—at the end of each *baktun*, and sometimes every ten or even five years—it might be supposed that Maya territory would be the archaeologist's paradise, with all problems of chronology solved in advance by the builders of the monuments themselves. This is certainly true in matters of relative chronology, since we can be certain that a stela dated 9.0.0.0.0 is ten *katun* earlier than a stela with the inscription 9.10.0.0.0, so that there is an interval of some two centuries between the two. But we are still left with problems of absolute chronology, of the correlation of Maya dates with our own system of dating.

The problem has been, and still is, the subject of keen debate. At first sight it ought to be a simple matter to establish how the Mayas of Yucatán in the 16th century dated such events as the arrival of the Conquistadors, the date of which is accurately fixed in our chronology. In fact, however, the later Mayas had abandoned the dating system of their ancestors, the so-called "Long Count", in favour of a "Short Count", an abridged system which was much less accurate. We must, therefore, proceed in stages: we must first discover in the historical texts a securely established European date (which will be expressed according to the Julian calendar), convert it to the Gregorian system, find its exact equivalent in the Short Count, and then establish the correlation between the Short Count and the Long Count.

The correlation most widely accepted by Maya scholars is that of Goodman, Martínez Hernández and Thompson, which starts from the equation 11.16.0.0.0, 13 *ahau* 8 *xul* = 14th November 1539 in the Gregorian calendar. The correlation established by H.J. Spinden would put all dates some 260 years farther back. The radiocarbon dating of three specimens of *chicozapote* wood from a panel found at Tikal bearing the date 9.15.0.0.0 produces results which appear to favour Spinden's theory; for according to the Goodman-Martínez-Thompson correlation the date inscribed on the panel is equivalent to 30th June 741, whereas radiocarbon dating gives dates of 481, 469 and 433, with a possible error of 120 years.

If, however, the generally accepted correlation is rejected we come up against other problems; for the Maya classic period would then end about the middle of the 7th century of our era instead of about the year 900, and we should be faced with a gap of more than two centuries which it would be difficult to fill. We should either have to suppose that the classic Maya civilisation had lasted for 250 years after the period when it ceased erecting stelae and carving inscriptions, or arbitrarily extend the Toltec period, or insert two additional centuries between the end of the Toltec period in Yucatán and the Spanish conquest—theories which are all in contradiction with the body of known facts. Most scholars prefer, therefore, to question the validity of the radiocarbon dating, at least in this particular instance. It is observed, reasonably enough, that this method can give the age of wood with fair accuracy but does not tell us how old the wood was when it was carved; and it may well be that the wood in question, which is of extreme hardness, was preserved for many years before being used.

In this book, therefore, we shall adopt the Goodman-Martínez-Thompson system for correlating Maya and European dates. A stela has recently been reported from Tikal with the date 8.12.14.8.15, which would take it back to the year 292 of our era. Apart from this the oldest known dates are those on the Leyden Plate (320) *(Plates 67–68)* and on Stela 9 at Uaxactún (328). The latest dates of the classic period are the end of the third *katun* of the tenth *baktun* (10.3.0.0.0, 889 A.D.), which we find carved at Uaxactún, Xultún and Xamantún, and the year 909 A.D. on a jade pectoral from Tzibanché. The Maya classic period thus lasted rather more than six hundred years.

Little progress has been made with the decipherment of Zapotec inscriptions. The stelae at Monte Albán appear to bear chronological and mathematical signs, dates based on a divinatory calendar of 260 days, and symbols of the solar year, which is represented by a kind of capital A. This glyph representing the year is also found at Teotihuacán and in the Mixtec manuscripts. Other symbols carved on the stelae seem to be connected with proper names or place names. We are still unable, however, to date the Zapotec monuments from the inscriptions. We are no better off at Teotihuacán, where the hieroglyphs are few in number and are found on small objects rather than on monuments. They are of a type very similar to those used in Zapotec writing, the figures being given according to the Maya system.

Nor does the script used at Xochicalco, a town in the state of Morelos on the western slope of the high plateau, which was at its peak between the 7th and 10th centuries, enable us to date the monuments found there. The hieroglyphs are similar in form to those used at Monte Albán, and the use of bars and dots for figures recalls the Maya system. The builders of Xochicalco were undoubtedly concerned with chronological calculations, for one of the carvings on the principal pyramid contains signs and figures belonging to two different scripts and calendar systems, as if seeking to establish a correlation between systems belonging to two distinct traditions. The fact that at Xochicalco the number 5 is usually represented by a bar in accordance with the Maya and Zapotec systems, but occurs at least once in the form of the Toltec five-not symbol, shows that this civilisation formed a transition between the classic era and the later period.

Chronological inscriptions are much less frequently found at Tula than in the Maya cities, but a few examples are known. Their characteristic features—the absence of the bar representing the figure 5, the absence of a cartouche round the glyphs, the realistic representation of the symbols—are identical with those of the Mixtec script and the script used at a later date by the Aztecs. The calendars of these various peoples had a common basis, a simplified form of the Maya Long Count. Each day was identified, as in the Maya system, by reference to the ritual calendar of 260 days and the solar calendar of 365 days. As a rule, however, the month was not specified, only the year being given. Each year was known by the number and the name of its first day. Since there was a series of thirteen figures and only four names[6] could be given to the first day of the year, the same "year bearer" (initial date) recurred only every 52 years (4 × 13). To the ancient Mexicans this 52-year cycle was charged with such cosmic and religious significance that they did not scruple to adjust their history in order to force events into their proper place in this framework. Thus the traditions about the Toltecs tell us that the town of Tula was founded in the year "1 Flint" (856) and was abandoned in the year 1168, which was also "1 Flint"—i.e., exactly six times 52 years later. Similarly the birth of the divinised king-priest Quetzalcoatl, the "Feathered Serpent", is dated to the year "1 Reed" (947), and his flight and mysterious disappearance to "1 Reed" (999), 52 years later. According to a widely believed legend he was due to return to Mexico in a "1 Reed" year; and it chanced that Cortés and his companions arrived in 1519, also a "1 Reed" year, coming from the "red country" to the east to which the Feathered Serpent was supposed to have gone. Thus at first the Mexicans, including even the Emperor Moctezuma, believed that these beings from another world were divine personages, messengers sent by Quetzalcoatl himself.

Even though Toltec history was adapted to some extent to fit into the framework of the 52-year cycles, it is nevertheless clear that in ati broad lines the native chronology is reliable, and that the Toltec civilisitson can be dated between the years 850 and 1170.

The Mixtecs of Oacaxa, those incomparable craftsmen and illuminators of manuscripts, recorded the history of their tribe in detai lfrom the establishment of the Tilantongo dynasty in 692 to the Spanish conquest. Their

[6] The number of days in the year, disregarding the five unlucky days, is 360, which is divisible by 20. Accordingly the first of the five intercalary days (which the Mayas called *uayeb* and the Aztecs *nemontemi*) has the same sign as the first day of the year; but since there are four other extra days the first day of the following year moves down five places compared with the year before; and since 20 divided by 5 is 4, there are only four signs which can be "year bearers". In the Aztec period these four signs were *acatl* (reed), *tecpatl* (flint), *calli* (house) and *tochtli* (rabbit).

splendid Codices (Becker, Nuttall *(Plate 138)*, Vindobonensis, Bodley, Selden) give us a profusion of circumstantial information about events in Oaxaca over a period of more than eight centuries, with an encyclopaedic wealth of detail on the customs, funeral practices, religious rites, clothing, weapons and music of the Mixtecs.

Each individual mentioned in these records usually had two names—a proper name such as, for example, "Jaguar's Claw" and a "calendric name" consisting of a date, which might be the date of his birth or of an important event in his life. Several Mixtec manuscripts record the glorious and eventful career of a national hero whose calendric name was "8 Deer", and who seems to have lived from 1011 to 1063, a period of exactly 52 years—for the Mixtec historians also adjusted their facts on occasion. His father was called "5 Alligator", his mother "9 Eagle". From the age of eight onwards he was engaged in warlike exploits, and in later years we encounter him at his devotions, playing the ball game, and of course making war. Between the ages of 21 and 30 he conquered twenty-six towns and villages. As his renown grew he gained the right to wear a turquoise nose ornament, which was presented to him, in the course of a solemn ceremony, by a priest who pierced his nasal septum with a bone awl. We then have a whole series of pictures showing him in conference with high dignitaries, negotiating and concluding treaties, and taking part in sacrifices. At the age of 40 he married a girl called "13 Snake", by whom he had a son, "6 House". Finally, on his fifty-second birthday, he died on the stone of sacrifice; and the scribe gives us a detailed picture of the scene, with "8 Deer" lying on the stone and the priest plunging his flint knife into the victim's breast.

The peoples of the central plateau belonging to the Nahuatl language family, including the Aztecs, recorded the history of their tribes and their cities by methods similar to those of the Mixtecs. The Aztecs put their departure from Aztlán, their legendary place of origin, in the year "1 Flint", or 1168—the date of the fall of Tula. This at any rate is the likeliest

102

103

104

106

1

←108, 109

112

113

114

115 116 117

8

19

← 120

121

122

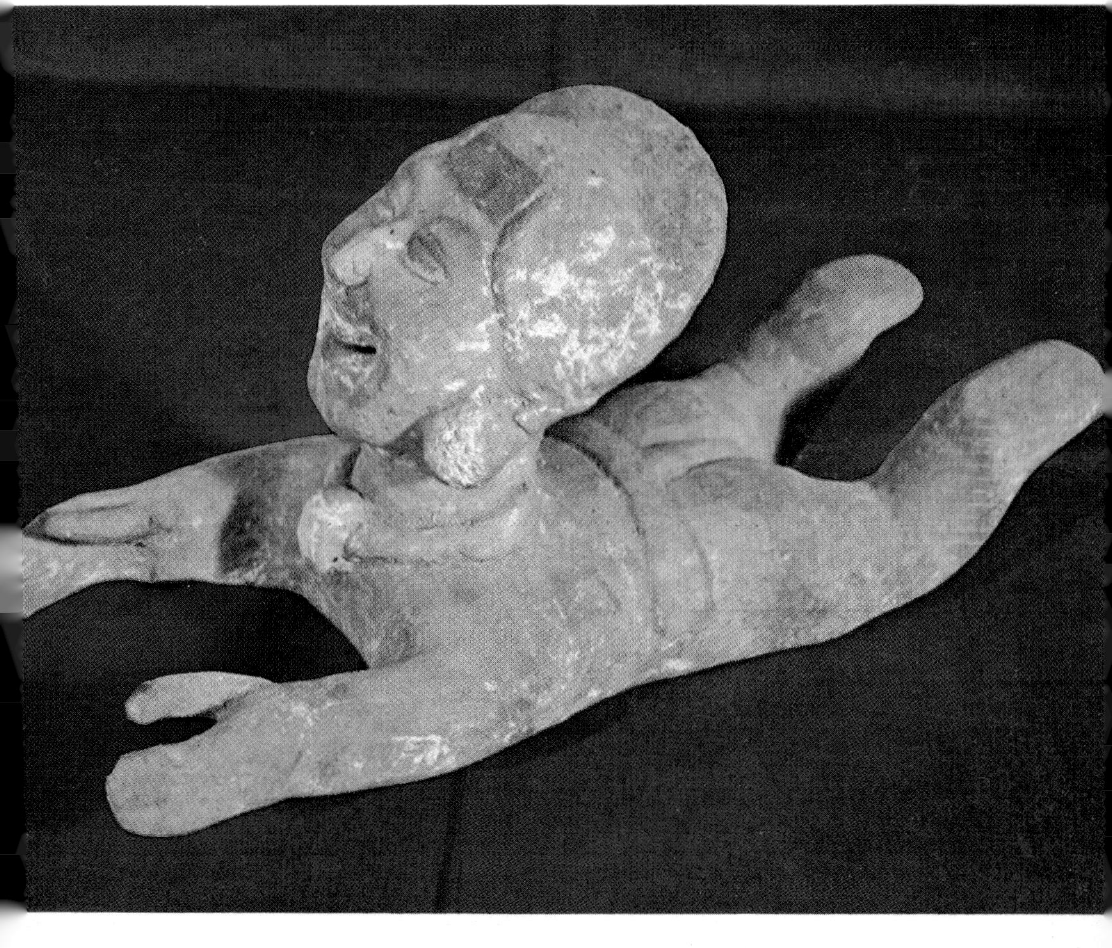

123

124

of the possible alternatives—for, as a result of the ambiguity created by the recurrence of the same dates every 52 years, some chronicles date the beginning of the great migration to the year 1064. The Aztecs were sure that their ancestors had stayed at Aztlán for more than a thousand years before setting out on their travels. The *Codex of 1576*, in the Boturini-Aubin-Goupil collection, records the long southward journey of the Aztecs and the tribulations they suffered until the foundation of their town—a wretched village of reed huts in the midst of the marshes—in 1325. The first "New Fire" ceremony, which marked the completion of the "year bundle" at the end of each cycle, was celebrated in the year "2 Reed"—1195; the last took place in 1507, twelve years before the arrival of the Conquistadors.

Like the Mayas, though with less regularity and less ostentation, the Aztecs commemorated important events in bas-relief carvings. Thus, for example, we have a dated stela, now in the National Museum in Mexico City, showing the Emperor Tizoc (*d.* 1486) and his successor Ahuitzotl inaugurating the great *Teocalli*, the temple of Uitzilopochtli and Tlaloc, in the year "8 Reed"—1487.

The date of the surrender of the Emperor Cuauhtemotzin, which delivered Mexico City into the hands of Cortés, is exactly known—"1 Snake" day in the year "3 House", or 13th August 1521. Here, at any rate, we have none of the difficulty we encounter in attempting to establish a correlation between native and European dates in Yucatán.

A word may be added on the Aztec system of writing as it existed at the time of the Conquest. Based on similar principles to the Maya script, though much less stylised and abstract, it represented a compromise between pictographic writing (the representation of scenes and objects), ideographic writing, and phonetic writing. We can regard as ideograms, for example, the hieroglyphs representing the twenty names of days, materials of practical use or intrinsic value such as flint, turquoise or gold, or ideas like war, night, and so on. But many signs, though representing particular objects, were also used to denote the sound of a syllable or group of syllables, with no reference to their original meaning. For example, the character representing "teeth", *tlan-tli*, denotes the suffix *-tlan* in place names, the glyph for "water", *a-tl*, represents the sound *a*, a stone *(te-tl)* indicates the syllable *te*, and a flag *(pan-tli)* the syllable *pan*. By combining these signs in the manner of a rebus the Aztec scribes were able to write the names of people or places—for example the name of the Emperor Itzcoatl (a snake, *coatl*, bristling with obsidian spikes, *itz-tli*), or of the town of Quauhtitlan (a tree, *quau-itl*, with teeth, *-tlan*).

Thus through all their varying forms—forms which, on the whole, show a remarkable continuity—the writin gsystems and chronology of the Mexican civilisations remain characteristic features of these civilisations from their birth to their final disappearance, during a period of over fifteen hundred years, and provide valuable answers to some of the archaeologist's problems. As we have seen, there are still many gaps and uncertainties in our knowledge, and some points of controversy; but we have nevertheless ample material to give us a clear picture of the general chronological framework.

Relations between Different Civilisations

We have already referred more than once to the problems posed by the relationships between the various civilisations of Mexico. None of these civilisations lived in a vacuum. In spite of the distances and the natural obstacles, and their lack of any means of transport, either pack animals or vehicles, the ancient Mexicans travelled about the country with surprising facility. War, trade and pilgrimage were the three main occasions for travel. The Toltecs who invaded Yucatán in the 11th century, the conquering Aztecs, the Mixtecs who gradually occupied the whole of the Oaxaca valley between the 11th and the 15th centuries, are examples of the armed migrations which brought so many different peoples into contact with one another. In general the waves of human movement travelled from north to south, from the northern steppes to the central plateaux and from there into Maya territory.

It was this mingling of peoples that gave some of the Mexican civilisations their composite character. Such, for example, were the Toltec civilisation, which combined the traditions of Teotihuacán with the new ideas brought by the first immigrants belonging to the Nahuatl family; the civilisation which the Toltecs later founded in Yucatán by amalgamating with the Maya population, producing a combination of cultures which is brilliantly displayed in the ornaments on the Temple of the Warriors at Chichén Itzá *(Plates 125, 126)*, partly Nahuatl (the Feathered Serpent) and partly Maya (the rain god Chac); the civilisation now called Mixteca-Puebla *(Plates 137–140, 143, 145–148)*, which mingles the religious conceptions and the plastic arts of the Mixtecs, the Nahua of Cholula and Tlaxcala, and other native peoples such as the Mazatecs of Teotitlán; and the Aztec civilisation itself, the crucible in which beliefs, customs and techniques from the Toltec tradition and a great variety of other peoples were combined to form a new alloy.

Some sanctuaries or sacred places, like the Great Cenote (a natural well) at Chichén Itzá, exercised a powerful attraction on pilgrims for many centuries; and no doubt the Itzá chose this site for their capital because of the sacred well. Similarly the Island of Sacrifice, off Veracruz, was frequented by worshippers bringing offerings from all over the country: the material found here includes valuable alabaster vases which evidently came from Oaxaca.

We know also that there was an active movement of trade throughout Mexico. The "archaic" craftsmen of Zacatenco and Ticomán were already importing shells from the Pacific or the Gulf Coast. At a later period, the magnificent painted vases of Teotihuacán are found in Guatemala. At Tikal, for example, a tomb dated to 457 contained a tripod jar with a conical lid, coated with painted stucco, and a later tomb yielded a bowl decorated with the face of Tlaloc, the rain god, and bearing the hieroglyph for the year.

It is clear that high quality pottery of this kind was already a favourite object of long distance trade. In the Teotihuacán period the most popular product was a type of orange ware of exceptional fineness, the source of which has not been determined: specimens of this are found throughout Mexico in levels belonging to the main classic period. It may have been manufactured at Teotihuacán.

At the end of the classic period, until about 1200, the fine pottery known as "plumbate ware", of excellent finish and great richness of form, was produced in the Soconusco province in the southern part of Maya territory. It too travelled widely, for specimens have been found in Guatemala, at Chichén Itzá, in Central America as far down as Nicaragua, and all over Mexico as far north as Nayarit.

At a still later period, immediately before the Conquest, we find the beautiful polychrome pottery of Cholula, a luxury product much sought after by kings and high dignitaries—the Emperor Moctezuma II used it at table—which was also widely distributed.

We have a detailed picture of the way of life and trading methods of the *pochteca*, the Aztec merchants who formed powerful guilds and had for all practical purposes a monopoly of external trade in Mexico City. Their caravans of porters travelled far to the south to sell the manufactured products of the capital (cloth, pottery, tools of flint and obsidian) and returned with raw materials from the Hot Lands (precious feathers, gold dust and jade).

But in this field many things are still obscure. Where, for example, did the builders of Teotihuacán come from, with their splendidly refined architecture and their essentially agricultural religion? Their city was built in the semi-desert conditions of the high plateau, at an altitude of 6500 feet, and we learn from their frescoes that their principal deity was the god of water and rain, and that they valued tropical products such as cacao, rubber, and the plumage of tropical birds. Had they come from the east, from the coastal area? Certainly some of the decorative elements in the temples, with their interlaced volutes, are very reminiscent of the style found at El Tajín *(Plates 108, 109)*. May it be that the priestly aristocracy of Teotihuacán originally came from the warm and luxuriant lands of the Coast, and held sway over a population of native peasants—probably the Otomi, a very ancient tribe belonging to the central plateau? But here, unfortunately, we are reduced to pure hypothesis.

Another problem in the same field is that of establishing the extent of Huaxtec influence on the civilisations of the central plateau. This people was distantly related to the Mayas, but must have been separated from the other tribes belonging to the same family before the birth of Maya civilisation. In their isolated position on the Coast and in the mountains of the north-east they pursued a development of their own, of which little is so far known because of the limited amount of excavation carried out in this area. It is interesting to note that according to Toltec tradition they had played a part in the fall of Tula; for it was the love of a daughter of the last Toltec king, Huemac, for a Huaxtec that caused the civil war which led to the fall of the city. In the Aztec period the Indians of the central plateau borrowed from the Huaxtecs the worship of the goddess of love and of sin, Tlazolteotl, certain characteristics of the wind god, and other features. Conversely we can see from the small quantity of Huaxtec sculpture and wall painting we possess that this people was strongly influenced at different periods by the civilisations of the high plateau.

Relations with North and South America

The area occupied by the Mexican civilisations was cut off from the main bulk of North America by a belt of steppe and desert. This did not, however, prove an insuperable obstacle, as is demonstrated by the extraordinary migration of the great Nahuatl or Uto-Aztec ethnic and linguistic family, which came from the present state of Utah and played a leading part in the history of Mexico from at least the 9th century.

It is clear that people and objects and influences must have travelled from north to south, and also in the reverse direction. Maize, which originally came from the Hot Lands of southern Mexico and Guatemala, was cultivated by the Indians of the southern United States. Obvious Mexican influences can be seen in the Hohokam tribe of Arizona, who played the ball game, for example, after the fashion of the Mayas and the other civilised peoples of Mexico.

Communications along the eastern coast of the Gulf of Mexico between what we now know as Texas and the other southern States on the one hand and the Huaxtec area on the other were relatively easy. The artificial eaathen mounds found all over the Mississippi and Ohio valleys contain an rbundance of objects, some of which—for example engraved shells—are very closely related in technique and decoration to specimens from Mexico, in particular the engraved shells of the Huaxtecs. The Indians of Georgia and Carolina had as their characteristic weapon a kind of scimitar-shaped wooden club which we find very accurately depicted in Huaxtec drawings and in certain manuscripts from Oaxaca. And we have already noted the similarity between the mounds themselves and the Huaxtec tumuli, the *yácatas* of Michoacán and primitive types of pyramid like that at Cuicuilco.

In this field there is undoubtedly a wide and exciting area for research; and this is true also of the relations between Mexico and South America.

The difference between the advanced civilisations of Andean America and Mexico are sufficiently obvious. The Peruvians domesticated certain ani; mals (the llama and alpaca, for example) which were unknown in Mexico- they cultivated the potato; and they had mastered the craft of goldsmith's work before the beginning of our era. The decorative styles, the pottery and the textiles of Chavín, Tiahuanaco, Nazca and other areas developed with magnificent vigour and originality. On the other hand, in spitc of the complexity of the political organisation of the Inca Empire, the Peruvians had no system of writing, and their chronological and astronomical knowledge remained rudimentary.

Nevertheless a considerable body of evidence has been accumulated pointing to long-continued trading relations between Mexico and Peru. Paul Rivet's work on the metallurgy of gold and its alloys, and of copper and bronze, shows that these complex techniques must have been introduced into Mexico by the Peruvians. It is significant that gold—which apart from one exceptional case (at Copán) is completely absent from Maya territory during the classic period—should not have made its appearance in Yucatán until the Toltec period, in the form of round plaques which were probably imported from Panama; and along the Pacific coast, and in the mountains of Oaxaca which lie inland from the coast, gold and silver working made a late appearance about the 10th century, soon to be followed by copper and bronze working. From this area it spread on the one hand into Michoacán by way of the Balsas valley, and on the other on to the central plateau, where the Aztecs became masters of the goldsmith's craft. And in this case it is not merely a matter of a few objects imported from Central America, as with the Mayas, but of the working of locally extracted ore.

The techniques employed in Mexico are the same as those found in Peru, in every detail (for example the chemical process known as "colouring" which gives an alloy of gold and copper the appearance of pure gold). The jewellery of Monte Albán is of distinctively Mixtec style and workmanship, but it includes a diadem with a gold plume which is an exact copy of a type commonly found in Peru. The Mixtec gold trinkets, the gold and silver tweezers for the removal of hair used by the Tarascans of Michoacán, the small copper axes which served as money—all these take us back to Inca models.

Other significant facts have been noted by archaeologists: for example a stone slab found at Placeres del Oro in the state of Guerrero is carved with figures of stylised felines very similar to the felines of Chavín in Peru. A resemblance has also been noted between the decorative motifs on certain Mixtec vases (fishes and snakes) and those found on vases from the coastal area of Peru. Some typically Peruvian types of pottery like the double jars with a stirrup spout are found only sporadically in Mexico, but—significantly—always in areas like Michoacán and Oaxaca.

Conversely, when we examine certain terracotta figurines and seals *(pintaderas)* from the coast of Ecuador (Esmeraldas) we are struck by their resemblance to similar objects from Mexico.

The existence of trading relations between Peru and Mexico is attested at the beginning of the 16th century: Pizarro's pilot, Bartolomé Ruiz de Estrada, records that he met, north of the Equator, one of the large sailing rafts used by Inca traders, heading north with a cargo of gold and silver, pottery and cloths. These goods were no doubt to be exchanged for a particular type of shell, not found in Peru, which was gathered to the south of Acapulco in Mexico. No doubt, too, this trade had been going on for many centuries. The ability of these large rafts *(balsas)* to sail long distances in the open sea has been demonstrated in our own day by Thor Heyerdahl's daring voyage on the "Kon-Tiki" from Peru to Polynesia.

126→

128

130→

129

132

133

134, 135→

The two civilised worlds of ancient America, Mexico and Peru, were thus not completely cut off from one another; but the detailed pattern of their relationships is almost entirely unexplored.

Relations with Other Continents

Still more enigmatic and fascinating is the question of possible relations between the civilisations of Mexico and the old world. Even discounting the wilder theories about Atlantis and the "lost continent of Mu", we are left with a number of similarities noted by scholars which cannot be explained away as mere chance resemblances.

As early as 1896 Edward B. Tylor compared the Mexican game of *patolli* with the game of *pachisi* found in Asia Minor and South-East Asia, noting that both were games of chance with similar rules and, significantly, that both were based on a cosmic symbolism. Fritz Graebner and Carl Hentze drew attention to similar elements in the ritual calendars of the Mayas and Mexicans on the one hand and of China and Java on the other, and in the symbolism of the dragon and the serpent. The religious architecture of Cambodia, with its temples built on the summit of pyramid-shaped structures several stories high, recalls the corresponding buildings of the Mayas and other Mexican civilisations, though the monuments of Angkor belong only to the 9th and 10th centuries of our era, much later than the temples of Tikal and Palenque *(Plates 56–64)*: the chronological difficulty thus seems insurmountable.

In the excellent series of studies he carried out over a period of thirty years from 1924 onwards Paul Rivet sought to identify all the anthropological, linguistic and ethnographical data in America, and particularly in South America, for which an Oceanian origin might be suggested; and the evidence he collected from the study of man and his activities, as well as from botany and comparative pathology, is too substantial to leave any room for doubt about the existence of similarities between the two sides of the Pacific. Paul Rivet's theories, like the theories about relations between Asia and America, were fiercely disputed by most scholars, but they are now attracting lively interest. Thus the 29th International Congress of Americanists (New York, 1949) discussed the whole problem of relationships between ancient America and the civilisations of Asia and Oceania. The Austrian ethnologist Robert von Heine-Geldern and the American archaeologist Gordom Ekholm have stressed the significance of certain parallels in art and in symbolism, such as the conventional representation of the water lily in the Toltec-Maya carvings and the Indian convention found at Amaravati, the cult of the jaguar, the legendary Chinese *T'ao-t'ieh* and the monstrous figures of Mexico, the ornamental volutes found in Chou bronzes and in the art of the Gulf Coast, etc. They also argue that it was perfectly possible for ships from southern Asia to reach the west coast of Mexico; and Rivet similarly maintained, with justification, that the hardy seamen of Malaya and Polynesia, who were able to sail to Hawaii and Easter Island, might well have reached the American continent.

It is not, of course, suggested that any particular civilisation was brought from Asia or Oceania and established ready made on the soil of America. In all essentials the Indian civilisations of Mexico, as of Peru, were the personal creation of peoples who had come from Asia twenty or twenty-five thousand years before our era, when they were still in a stage of cultural development of Palaeolithic type. These "Indians" would undoubtedly bring with them certain ideas and traditions which would explain some of the similarities which have been observed; but, starting from a very primitive level of development, they had to invent for themselves the techniques of agriculture, building and metal-working, the arts and crafts they practised, a system of writing, and so on. They were ignorant of the use of iron and the wheel. Moreover the very individual hieroglyphic and chronological systems of Mexico suggest that they were evolved by these Indian peoples in their new country and were not borrowed from anywhere else.

In the present state of knowledge, however, the origins of the advanced civilisations of Mexico, and of the Olmec civilisation in particular, still remain mysterious. We certainly cannot exclude the possibility that particular cultural features may have travelled from the Old World to the New.

What can be deduced from the studies mentioned above is that certain common elements are found throughout a circum-Pacific complex which takes in America, South-East Asia and Oceania, and that it was technically possible for the people of Asia or of Malaya and Polynesia to sail from one side of the Pacific to the other. For the moment we cannot go any farther than this: we have no answer to the problem. Much painstaking research, detailed analytical study, and excavation will be required for its solution—if indeed a solution is ever found.

THE METHODS OF MEXICAN ARCHAEOLOGY

III

Captain Antonio del Río prided himself, in the report which has already been mentioned, on having spared no effort at Palenque to ensure that "there should not remain a single door or window but has been cleared, not a wall but has been pierced, not a room, a corridor, a courtyard or an underground passage but has been dug to a depth of two or three fathoms." It need hardly be said that archaeological methods have changed considerably since then. The practice of haphazard and often destructive excavation, and of the hasty "creaming off" of sites to supply museums and private collections with valuable pieces has been succeeded by properly organised research. (In spite of this the looting of tombs still continues in certain regions, for example in the Colima and Nayarit areas, where thousands of terracotta figurines and jars have been extracted) *(Plates 7, 16, 18, 21, 25–27).*

Archaeology in Mexico, as in other countries, is not so much a single science as a synthesis of sciences and techniques all directed towards the same end—the reconstitution of the ancient civilisations in all their aspects, including not only their material culture, their art and their religion, but also their succession in time, their interconnections, and the influence they exerted on one another.

Archaeology thus calls on half a dozen different sciences in carrying out its research and formulating its conclusions. Geology enables us to study the environment, to determine the age of particular natural features, and sometimes to establish the date at which phenomena like a volcanic eruption or a flood took place, leaving traces which can be associated with a particular human settlement. Somatic anthropology studies fossilised bones, compares ethnic types, and makes comparisons also with the native races of the present day. Linguistics and philology have an essential contribution to make in a country which was occupied by civilised peoples with a system of writing, and in which languages such as Maya and Nahuatl are still spoken. Ethnography is brought in to interpret the remains of the lost civilisations of the past on the basis of comparisons with modern or recent cultures. The comparative history of religions throws light on many aspects of these ancient civilisations which were so powerfully structured by their beliefs and their rituals. And finally sociology makes it possible to interpret their buildings, their burial practices and their paintings or carvings in terms of social or even political structures.

The ideal archaeologist ought thus to be an Admirable Crichton, excelling in every discipline. He must have a thorough grasp of the complex techniques involved in excavation and its immediate follow-up; he must be an architect, familiar with the building methods in use in each period, and able to recover and re-create the appearance of fallen buildings; he must be a specialist in pottery, capable of classifying and comparing systematically the countless vases, statuettes, figurines and sherds which every excavation brings to light; he must even, nowadays, be a physicist using radioactivity (carbon 14) to date his sites, and a botanist and zoologist seeking to identify pollens, seeds, plants, animals' bones and shells.

In fact, the increasing scale and complexity of the disciplines and techniques involved makes archaeology, of necessity, a matter of teamwork. All the experts concerned work together—some in the field, others in laboratories, museums and libraries—patiently fitting together the pieces of the jigsaw which will build up into the picture of a site, a town, a people or a period.

An extraordinarily fruitful method in Mexican archaeology has been the systematic comparison of the buildings, the iconography and the material excavated with the ancient literature, both native and Spanish. The interpretation of carvings, statues and engraved jade objects in the light of information gleaned from the works of such writers as Sahagún or Ixtlilxochitl, Bishop Landa or a nameless "jaguar priest" of Yucatán, has given us a profound insight into the structure and the modes of thought of these ancient societies.

The actual techniques of excavation are of course basically the same as in other parts of the world. It is scarcely necessary to stress the fundamental importance of stratigraphy. In Mexico, as in other countries, successive human settlements have been superimposed on one another, each period building on the ruins of the one before. By means of carefully planned trenching it is possible to identify layers of different thickness and varying composition belonging to different periods and subdivisions of periods, which provide the basis for a relative chronology. The method most commonly adopted is to dig trenches or shafts some 8 feet wide, carefully removing the soil in successive layers. The layers may be either of a given standard depth of say 8 inches, or an attempt may be made to distinguish them by their colour and texture or by the nature of any objects found in them. By this means a section is obtained going from ground level down to undisturbed soil.

The stratigraphy of the accumulation of refuse which any human settlement leaves scattered about on the ground is, of course, of a very different nature from the stratigraphy of tombs and buildings. In the former case we are concerned with objects discarded by the occupants, particularly cooking utensils; in the latter with the finest achievements of a particular civilisation. As examples of the second category—out of a host of others which might be quoted—we may take the 170 tombs of Monte Albán, the tombs of Kaminaljuyú, the splendid jade offerings of La Venta, and the many "caches" of objects of the highest quality which have been found in the Maya sanctuaries.

The study of pottery is an essential element in stratigraphical classification. While flint or obsidian tools show little variation over long periods, terracotta artefacts have three useful qualities: they are found almost everywhere from the beginning of the rudimentary cultures of the pre-classic era; even when reduced to sherds or *tepalcates* they withstand almost indefinitely the destructive forces of nature, retaining their distinctive characteristics (the type of clay used, the quality of the firing, the glaze, the incised or painted decoration, and so on); and the techniques, shapes and decoration vary from one people to another and from one period to another, providing a very reliable means of classifying cultures both in space and time. Thus, for example, the discovery of a figurine from Ticomán, a painted tripod from Teotihuacán *(Plates 38–40)*, a Huaxtec "teapot"-shaped vessel, a Maya vase of the classic period or a Mixtec vase decorated with mythological themes enables us to date a site or a tomb with great precision.

The eminent Maya scholar Sylvanus Morley said that pottery represented the best guide in the study of the development of a civilisation; and in fact it has been possible to establish for the Maya civilisation a series of sequences, both in Yucatán and Guatemala, which takes us through the whole history of these peoples from the pre-Maya formative period (Mamom and Chikanel pottery types) to the Toltec and Mexican periods, by way of the magnificent classic pottery of Tzakol (about 300–600) and Tepeu (about 600–900).

Styles of architecture also provide reliable criteria. Ancient Mexican architecture produced a range of variations on two themes which are found in every city—the pyramid and the palace; and each of the variations is characteristic of a particular civilisation and a particular period. The builders of Teotihuacán decorated the sides of their pyramids with horizontal friezes edged with stone slabs, and the staircase which climbed up the face started from a structure, also pyramidal in shape, built on to the face of the main pyramid in the middle of one of the sides. These features are characteristic of the architecture of Teotihuacán, and when we find them also at Kaminaljuyú in the highlands of Guatemala we can be sure, beyond any possibility of error, that the influence of Teotihuacán had been felt in this distant area on the central plateau—a conclusion which is confirmed by the pottery. Similarly Toltec architecture—in which temples and palaces are combined in a complex pattern of pillared halls round the pyramids, with staircases leading up to great doorways with lintels supported by feathered serpents—has such strikingly distinctive characteristics that we need only glance at photographs of Tula *(Plates 132, 133, 135)* or Chichén Itzá *(Plates 125, 126, 130, 131)* to see at once that these two towns, more than six hundred miles apart as the crow flies, were built under the direction of master builders who were inspired by the same ideas.

The nature of the ground and the climate, and the religious and funerary customs peculiar to each culture, may either complicate or facilitate the task of the archaeologist. Whereas in Peru the absolute aridity of the soil in the coastal areas has ensured the perfect preservation of the marvellous fabrics of Paracas and Nazca, for example, as well as many objects in wood, perishable substances have suffered grave deterioration from the heavy rains of central Mexico and still more from the extreme humidity of the classic Maya territory. Not a trace is left of the sumptuous cloaks pictured, for example, in the sculptures of Yaxchilán and the illuminated Codices. Of the ornaments of precious feathers which the ancient Mexicans prized so highly there remain only a few specimens, including in particular the famous *quetzalapanecayotl* in the Ethnographical Museum in Vienna, the magnificent headdress presented by Moctezuma to Cortés and sent by him to the Emperor Charles V *(Plate 177)*.

As for sculpture in wood, although relatively recent specimens from central Mexico (for example the splendid gongs and drums of Mexico City, Malinalco and Tlaxcala) have survived, the Maya wood carving which must have preceded the stone bas-reliefs is known only from the panels from Tikal which are now in the Ethnographical Museum in Basle *(Plates 69, 70)*—authentic masterpieces whose perfection arouses a pang of regret that so much similar work has been lost.

The information we can glean from the tombs varies according to the funeral practices of the different peoples. In many ancient civilisations the dead were surrounded in the tomb with a great variety of everyday articles or precious objects; other peoples practised cremation. Thus at Palenque a sarcophagus of the 7th century with fine carved decoration, accompanied by jade jewellery and stucco sculpture of the highest quality, was found in a concealed chamber under the Pyramid of the Inscriptions; at Monte Albán were found Zapotec tombs decorated with frescoes on religious themes and a Mixtec tomb containing fine gold jewellery; at La Venta a sarcophagus, jewellery and jade statuettes. But the gorgeous ceremonial garments, the feather ornaments and the jewellery worn by the emperors who ruled in Mexico City were reduced to ashes in the course of their solemn funeral ceremonies.

One other practice commonly adopted by the ancient Mexicans has been of great assistance to archaeologists—their habit of enlarging their pyramids by covering the existing structure with earth and stones in order to produce a new monument of increased size. If we drive a tunnel into a pyramid, therefore, we reach a succession of older pyramids, each fitted inside the other.

The Pyramid of the Sun at Teotihuacán *(Plate 41)* was built in a single operation, forming an enormous mass of 1,700,000 cubic yards of sun-dried brick and stone with a facing of stones and stucco; but the pyramid of Cholula, dedicated from a remote period to the cult of the Feathered Serpent, contains within it a sanctuary of the Teotihuacán period covered with successive layers belonging to later periods, and the Temple of Quetzalcoatl at Chichén Itzá *(Plate 130)* is built over an older and smaller pyramid which seems to have been dedicated to the Sun and contained in its sanctuary a magnificent stone throne in the form of a jaguar and a splendid mosaic symbolising the solar disc.

The pyramid of Tenayuca, six miles from Mexico City, was completed, in the form in which we see it today, in the Aztec period. It stands 60 feet high on a base 200 feet by 160, but the original structure was only 25 feet high on a base 100 feet by 40, and five later pyramids had successively been built on top of the first one. At the relatively recent period to which this monument belongs it is probable that the rebuilding took place every 52 years, on the occasion of the New Fire which marked the passage from one cycle to the next. On this theory, since the last New Fire was lit in 1507, the first pyramid must have been built in 1247. We may note in passing that this dating fits in with the traditional accounts which tell us that the first sanctuary at Tenayuca was built by "barbarians" speaking the Nahuatl language who arrived on the central plateau about the year 1200 and came under the civilising influence of Toltecs who were still living in this area.

The proper investigation of structures produced by the superimposition of work of different dates confronts the excavator with some delicate problems. It would be fatal to tunnel at random from the upper layers towards the lower, leading to the collapse of entire sections. It is necessary to proceed with great care, tackling the structure from the base, beginning with trenches and then starting to tunnel. When we encounter a wall or staircase we can then continue round the wall or up the staircase, cutting passages which must usually be strengthened like mine workings. At Cholula, for example, no less than five miles of passages have been cut through the pyramid since excavation began in 1931.

It is only when the exploration of a monument has been completed, and before consolidation and restoration have been carried out, that the excavators can drive a vertical shaft from the centre of the topmost platform down to virgin soil. They thus obtain a complete stratigraphical section, which allows them not only to establish the different building levels but to take samples of the materials used at each level, in particular of the pottery which is found mingled with the bricks and earth used for building up each successive structure.

The reader must not be alarmed by the reference to restoration. This is not a matter of arbitrarily rebuilding the structure, but of saving it from destruction; for the remains, stripped of their covering of earth and honeycombed with tunnels and trenches, would not long survive the effects of weathering. After consolidation, the object should be so far as possible to restore the original appearance of the structure. Often the outermost layer will have been almost entirely destroyed, and the aim must then be to preserve the level below this, leaving tunnels or shafts into the interior so that the visitor can see the earlier stages of construction. Sometimes parts of the structure may have fallen away in one piece, and all that is necessary is to return them to their original position: this was the case, for example, at Tula, where the Serpent Wall of the *Coatepantli (Plate 133)* had collapsed and was found lying in front of the remains. Sometimes, too, the size and shape of the fallen stones makes it possible to restore them with certainty to their former positions. Most of the Maya sanctuaries of the early period have preserved their roofs complete with the openwork "roof combs", or at least considerable parts of them. Most of the buildings of central Mexico, on the other hand, are roofless.

In Mexico City and the neighbouring towns and villages the celebration of the New Fire was accompanied by large-scale destruction of ordinary domestic pottery. The moment the flame of the new cycle had flared up on the summit of Mount Uixachtecatl, and it was certain that the end of the world had been postponed for at least another 52 years, pots, dishes, plates and vessels of all kinds were broken into fragments and each family equipped itself with a fresh stock. This custom has made it possible for archaeologists like George C. Vaillant to study huge accumulations of sherds and establish with certainty the development of pottery shapes and decorative styles half-century by half-century; and the results of these studies help to solve the chronological problems of any site yielding Aztec pottery of known types.

Finally the comparative study of the plastic arts, and in particular of sculpture, in which all the civilised peoples of antiquity excelled, can provide most valuable information about the development of these peoples, the influence of one people on another, and the content of their cultures—their system of symbols, their conception of the world and their social structure. The style characteristic of each civilisation is a reality which we can define, and a closer analysis makes it possible to establish, within each style, the variations peculiar to a particular period or a particular site. Thus we can distinguish at a glance between a classic Maya bas-relief and a piece of Aztec carving; and, more subtly, we can recognise the archaic features in the representations of human figures in the oldest carvings at Tikal, the increasing ease and freedom of Piedras Negras, the grace of the Palenque stucco work *(Plates 56, 57, 65, 66)*, the flamboyant art of Quiriguá. We see the rude vigour of Tula softened by contact with the Mayas in the Yucatec revival; then, in the period of decadence, we find at Mayapán the dreary repetition of stereotyped themes. And again we can watch the Aztec people, late arrivals and half barbarous at first, assimilating and at the same time transforming the Toltec tradition.

Along with the study of styles, however, archaeology must concern itself with the ideological and, where appropriate, the historical content of works of art. The carvings and wall paintings of Teotihuacán *(Plates 49, 54)*, the Maya cities, Monte Albán and Mexico City—to mention only a few sites—are a mine of information on the clothing, the weapons, the ritual and the astronomical knowledge of the ancient Indians. The Bonampak frescoes depict the hair styles, the dress and the jewellery worn by Maya men and women of the 7th century, their weapons, their musical instruments, their very fans and parasols. Nearer to us in time, the great solar disc of Mexico City is a record in stone of the cosmological ideas of the Aztecs and their conception of time: and the Stone of Tizoc recounts the conquests and victories of this Aztec ruler.

Thus archaeology in the widest sense of the term, calling on a range of associated disciplines, is seen to be an all-embracing "total history" which enables us, in spite of many gaps and uncertainties and large areas of total obscurity, gradually to reconstitute the past of a whole section of mankind.

PANORAMA OF MEXICAN ANTIQUITY

IV

The provisional results of the research carried out over the last century and more, but particularly within the last fifty years, give us a general view of the various civilisations which followed one another in Mexico. We must not forget that new discoveries may compel us to revise many ideas which are now accepted without question; and the following account must, therefore, be considered as no more than a stage in the advance of a science which has already made great progress and undergone great changes.

From the Neolithic Revolution to the Urban Revolution

We still know very little about the oldest phases of human settlement in Mexico. Between fifteen and twenty thousand years before our era parts of the country were occupied by tribes of hunters who used tools and weapons of flaked stone, as has been proved by the discoveries at Tepexpán and Santa Ana Ixtapán in the Valley of Mexico. It is probable that before the culture of the maize-growing farmers there was an earlier culture similar to that of the Basket Makers who lived in the southern United States. The gathering of wild plants—seeds, roots, and so on—must have developed before the regular growing of cultivated plants.

We know that the Aztecs gave the name of *Chichimeca* ("barbarians") to the nomadic peoples who at the beginning of the 16th century of our era occupied the mountains and great steppes of Mexico to the north of a line running roughly along the River Lerma from its mouth to Xocotitlán, and thereafter by way of the Otomi villages and townships of Xilotepec, Nopala and Zimapán to the Gulf at Tuxpan. These warlike hunting tribes were contained at the frontiers of the Aztec empire and the Tarascan kingdom of Michoacán. They did a certain amount of trade by barter with neighbouring villages, particularly with the Otomi people of Xilotepec. We know a good deal about these tribes, since both the Aztecs and later the Spaniards came up against their stubborn resistance. They were ignorant of agriculture (apart from a few semi-sedentary tribes near the frontier), of weaving and of the art of pottery. They lived by hunting and by gathering wild fruit. They used stone mortars to make flour from the fruit of the *mezquitl*, a plant of the mimosa family which grows profusely in this area. They clothed themselves in skins and lived in caves or primitive huts. Their time was spent roaming over the vast semi-desert areas in quest of game and plants for food, usually in small family groups which could more readily provide for their own requirements.

No doubt the pattern of life was broadly the same for the whole population of Mexico until 3000 or 2500 years before our era. The *Chichimeca* were, in effect, representatives of a Palaeolithic culture which had survived into more recent times and lived on alongside the great civilisations of later periods.

The introduction of maize and other cultivated plants characteristic of Mexican agriculture—beans, gourds, tomatoes, peppers—seems to have started from the "Hot Lands" of the tropical zone on the Gulf Coast and in Chiapas and Petén. Maize undoubtedly advanced from south to north. Cotton, cacao and rubber could not acclimatise themselves on the high plateau, and the cloths of this area were therefore made from agave fibres. At a later period a trade in cotton, cacao and rubber, as well as in the rich plumage of parrots, macaws and *quetzals*, developed on a considerable scale.

By analogy with the corresponding developments in the Old World about the year 6000 B.C. we can give the name of "Neolithic revolution" to the profound change which took place in Mexico roughly three thousand years later. An important difference between the two processes, however, is that the people of Mexico had no animals capable of being domesticated, such as cattle, goats, sheep, pigs, donkeys or horses. Accordingly they could not go in for stock rearing, they could not produce meat or milk, and they had no animals to harness to a plough or a cart or to use as beasts

136

137

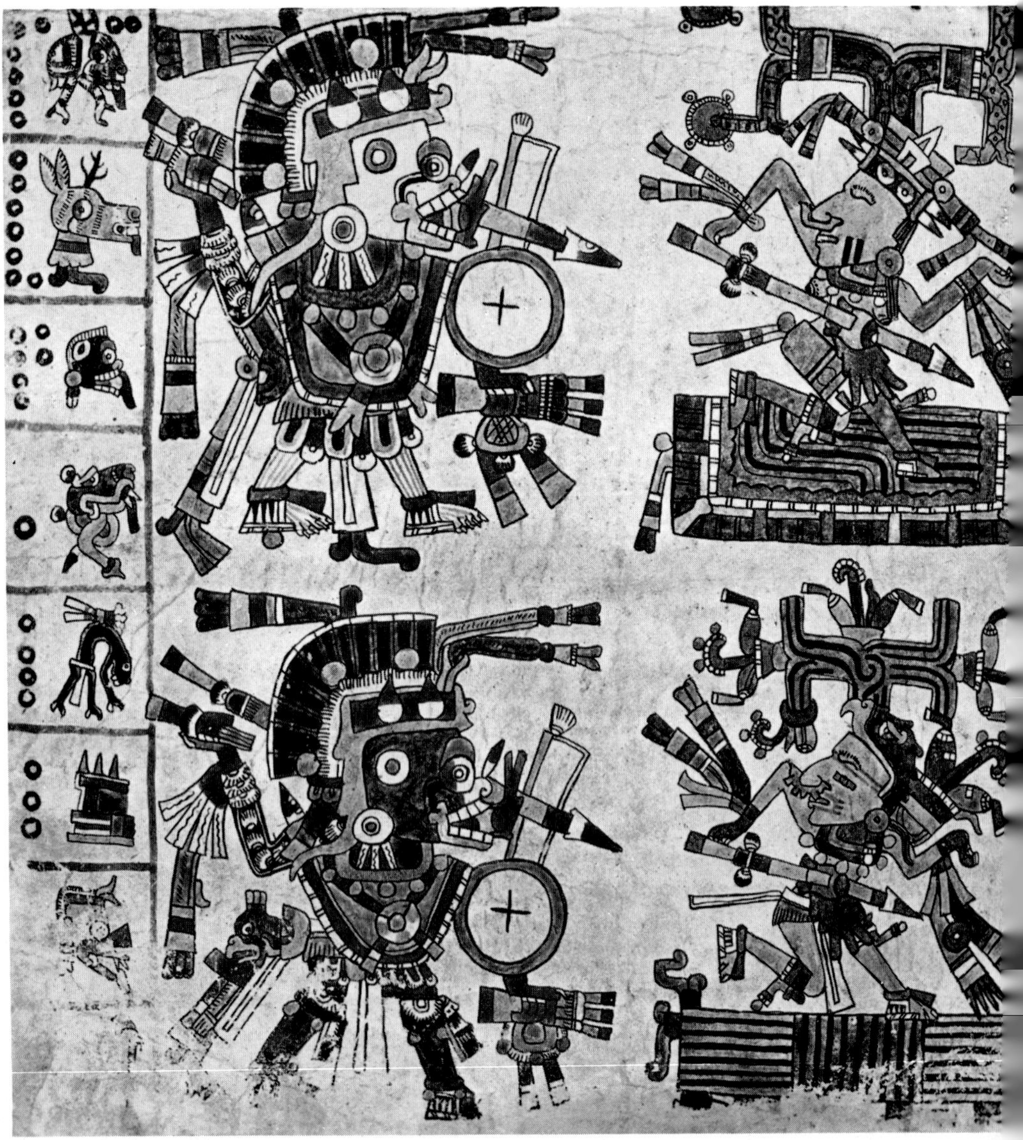

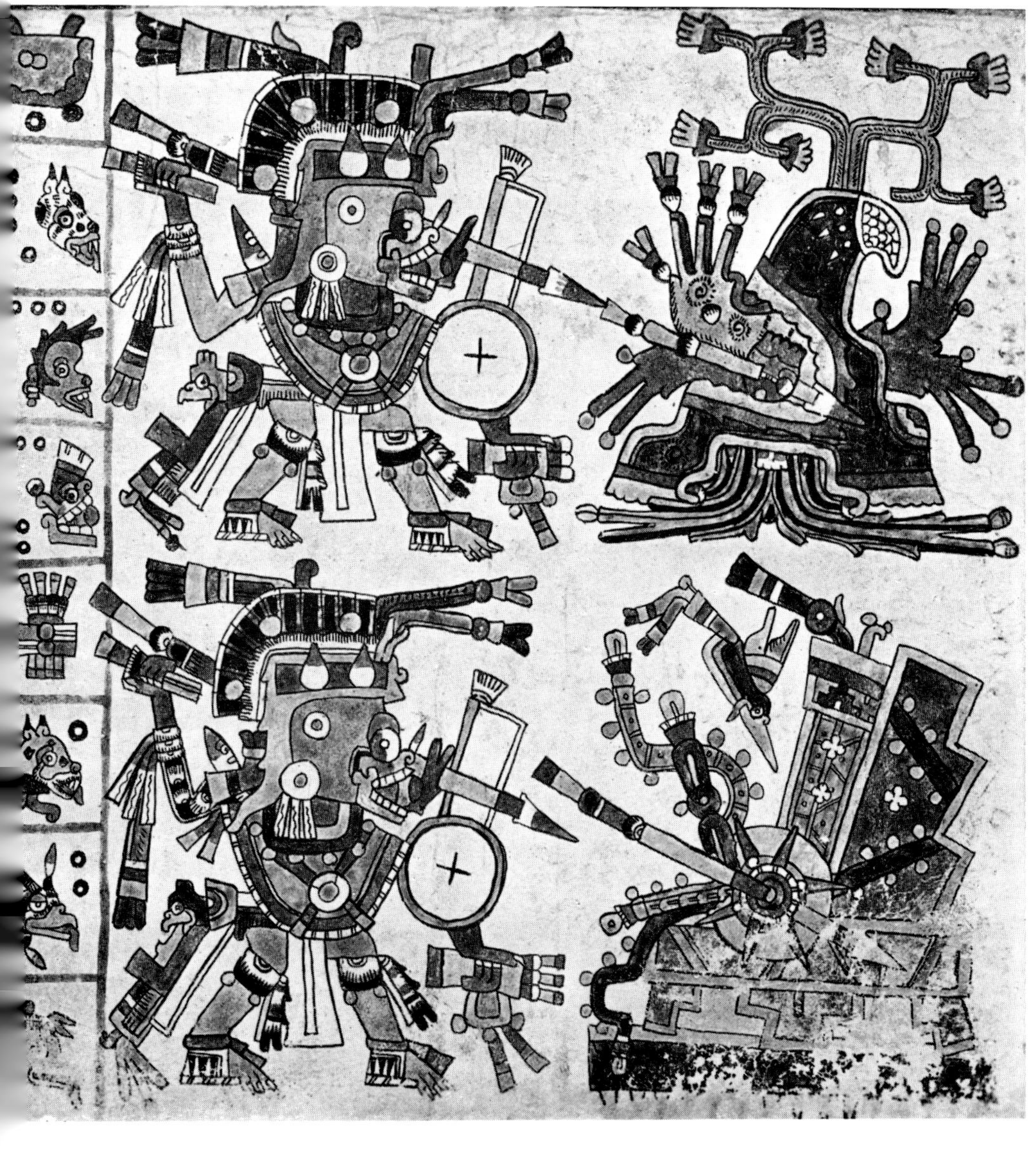

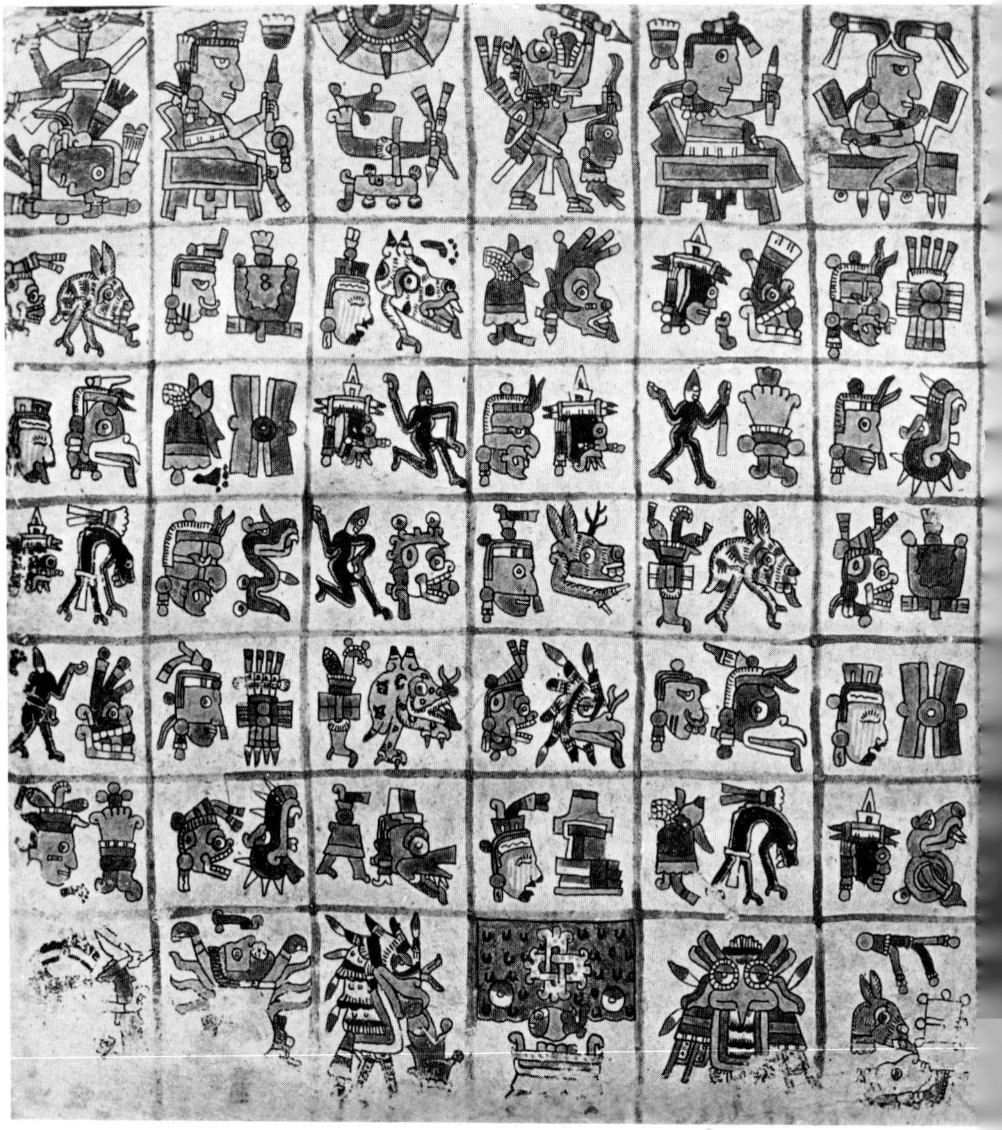

140

143 144→

145

147

146

148

of burden. The only animals they could rear were the dog and the turkey. But in maize they possessed one of the great cereals of the world, to be compared with wheat, barley and rice in importance. They also knew how to produce a fermented drink from the juice of the agave; and in this period, too, they discovered the arts of weaving and pottery.

The tribes now gave up their wandering habits and settled down in their villages to cultivate their fields. They did not, however, lose their taste for hunting, and at the time of the Conquest the Aztecs and their neighbours were still renowned as hunters and as great consumers of game. In the atmosphere of security created by successfully garnered harvests there grew up an organised collective life based on a hierarchical social structure. The wandering and insecure existence of the nomad, perpetually driven by hunger, gave place to the settled life of the peasant farmer. By the same token the small family groups came together, and clusters of permanent houses were built. The necessities of work in the fields, irrigation, and self-defence against covetous neighbours led to the development of an embryonic system of local government. By the pre-classic period the figurines found in the tombs, with their very elaborate hair styles, turbans and ornaments, suggest that these small rural communities had developed their own political hierarchy.

This village phase lasted nearly three thousand years on the central plateau, where we know most about it; but throughout the whole of the north-western area (Colima, Nayarit, Jalisco) it continued practically unchanged until the Spanish conquest. The Indians of this area, cut off from the great civilisations of Mexico, maintained the pre-classic Neolithic culture alongside the cities and empires which grew up elsewhere, just as the "barbarians" of the north continued in the Palaeolithic way of life. Their pottery is lively and spontaneous, and quite without any theological preoccupations.

Thus at the beginning of the 16th century the Aztec cities, the villages of the north-west and the hunting tribes of the north lived side by side, rather as if, on our own continent, the Romans, the Neolithic inhabitants of the lake villages and the cave dwellers of the Dordogne had all been living at the same time.

We can go farther, indeed, and observe that the village remained the fundamental unit of Indian life through all the vicissitudes of the great Mexican civilisations. Teotihuacán and Tula, Monte Albán and Mitla, Palenque and Uaxactún, Chichén Itzá and Uxmal—all these cities rose to greatness, shone with incomparable brilliance, and then, one after the other, disappeared. But all round them, caught up in their rivalries and subject to their authority, the villages stubbornly and unspectacularly survived. It was they who provided food for the cities, who supplied the labour force which built the pyramids. Successive waves of conquerors gained control over them and compelled them to pay tribute; and the Spaniards in turn, when they succeeded the Aztecs, behaved in exactly the same way.

The beginnings of urban life had appeared on the central plateau by the end of the pre-classic period. The population must have grown enormously as a result of the abundant food supply, and the villages began to develop into townships. The construction of the pyramid of Cuicuilco required a prolonged and organised building effort under the direction of architects (perhaps priests) who wielded sufficient authority to coordinate the work of an army of labourers and stone-masons; and the building of the Olmec pyramids, and in particular the transportation of their huge monoliths, cannot have been achieved without a political structure sufficiently complex and sufficiently well organised to mobilise the considerable labour force required.

The ancient Mexican city was above all a ceremonial centre made up of earthworks and buildings grouped round one or more temples, together with a variety of altars, stelae and carved monoliths. The first towns in this sense were the various Olmec centres, in particular La Venta. Thus the second revolution, the urban revolution, can be dated to the beginning of our era. The term of urban revolution seems entirely apt, for here, as in Mesopotamia and Egypt, the town was much more than an overgrown village. It was a quite new phenomenon: a cult centre, but also a centre of trade and a seat of authority, where the population of the surrounding area gathered to take part in religious rites, where they came to exchange their produce in the market, and where they acknowledged the spiritual or military authority of the rulers of the city. A centre for the development of new ideas, of the arts, of writing, of astronomical and mathematical speculation, the city dominated the landscape with its pyramids and palaces, and dominated men's minds with the forces of invention and discovery which flourished within its walls. Throughout the centuries the country was successively—or sometimes simultaneously—attracted and repelled by the town. Sometimes it supplied the town with its labour and its produce, and no doubt sent there also its best men; at other times it turned away from the town, or on occasion even rose in revolt against it.

The Classic Period

The cities of the classic period were Teotihuacán, Monte Albán, Tíkal, Uaxactún and the other great Maya cities. Broadly the practice of town dwelling arose, developed and died out throughout Mexico during the 1st millennium. The earliest Maya dates known (292 A.D. at Tikal, 320 on the Leyden Plate, 328 on Stela 9 at Uaxactún) are contemporaneous with the beginnings of Teotihuacán; the latest (785 at Palenque, 889 at Uaxactún) correspond to a period when the Teotihuacán civilisation had already faded, and lingered on, in a late form, only at the "colony" of Azcapotzalco. At Monte Albán Olmec influence was preponderant during the first two or three centuries of our era, and was still very evident until 500. The most flourishing period of Teotihuacán was from 400 to 700, of the Maya cities from 600 to 800, of Monte Albán (the classic Zapotec civilisation) from 500 to 1000. On the Gulf Coast, though we are not yet able to date El Tajín, it is very likely that the pyramid on this site belongs to the same period as the pyramids of Teotihuacán *(Plates 41, 108)*.

The great classic cities are distinguished from the Olmec towns by their area and by the number and scale of their buildings. Teotihuacán has a total area of two and three-quarter square miles, the Pyramids of the Sun and the Moon are respectively 210 and 140 feet high, the Avenue of the Dead is 1850 yards long. Scores of buildings survive, some of them undoubtedly dwelling houses: at Tlamimilolpa, for example, no fewer than 175 rooms have been counted. The Palace at Palenque *(Plates 56, 57, 60)*—where the only part cleared is what must have been the centre of the town—stands on a terrace some 330 feet by 230 and contains a range of rooms and galleries grouped round four patios and crowned by a three-storey tower—though the pyramids on which the temples are built are of relatively modest size, the largest standing no more than 70 feet high. The pyramids of Tikal reach a height of some 200 feet. At Copán in Honduras and at Uxmal in Yucatán the buildings stand in majestic groupings, excellently adapted to the nature of the ground and often of spectacular size. The "Governor's Palace" *(Plate 73)* and "Nunnery Quadrangle" at Uxmal and the Acropolis at Copán, with the skilfully planned harmony of their staircases, their courtyards, their pyramids and their ball courts, are the work of architects with a complete mastery of their craft. The same technical skill is shown at Monte Albán, a Sacred Mountain which was completely remodelled by the successive generations of builders who erected their temples and palaces and dug their tombs here.

Contemplating the remains of the classic cities, we can still say with substantial truth that their main function was to serve as a ceremonial centres, but we must at once add two qualifications. In the first place the huge horizontal structures which we call "palaces", and which are clearly distinct from the sanctuaries, must have been the residences of high dignitaries, places of assembly, and military headquarters. Secondly, there must certainly have been dwelling houses built round the temples and the palaces, usually of sun-dried brick on the high plateau or of wood or other flimsy material in the tropical areas. On the basis of comparison with the cities of the Aztec period such as Tenochtitlán we may reasonably conclude that the dwellings of the rulers of the city, the priests and the military leaders, were built as close as possible to the centre, and that the houses of the ordinary people were in the outer districts which straggled out into the countryside.

These great cities of the 1st millennium differ from one another in the style of their buildings and their sculpture. There is a striking diversity between the huge and massive pyramids of Teotihuacán and the pointed pyramids of Tikal, between the riot of carving on the friezes, the panels and the lintels of Palenque and Yaxchilán and the austere sobriety of Monte Albán, between the geometric decoration of the façades in Yucatán and the flamboyant bas-reliefs of Copán. But the various classic civilisations have also many features in common, and these common features are of decisive importance. In spite of the variety of local styles the fundamental conceptions of the architecture are everywhere very similar; the same hieroglyphic script was used, to a much greater extent among the Mayas than at Teotihuacán or even among the Zapotecs, but based everywhere on the same principles; and the reckoning of time was also on the same basis everywhere. We may note that the art of writing and a system of chronology were known to the Olmecs, who in this respect may be considered the true forerunners of the classic civilisations; but in the present state of knowledge it does not appear that this enigmatic people ever applied architectural techniques like the corbelled vault of the Mayas or the colonnades of the Zapotecs.

From this point of view we may say that the Olmecs represent a transitional phase—that they were both the last pre-classic and the first classic civilisation.

When we compare the art of the pre-classic villagers with that of the Olmecs and of the great cities we cannot but be struck by the fact that the former is spontaneous and naturalistic, the latter elaborate, hieratic and steeped in religious conceptions. Preoccupations of this kind are not, of course, totally lacking in pre-classic art. The female figurines which have been found in large numbers in excavations in the Valley of Mexico and farther north (the "pretty ladies" of Chupícuaro) may be connected with a fertility cult. The two-headed figurines and the curious figures, half human being, half skeleton, found in the late phase at Ticomán and Tlatilco no doubt refer to myths about the duality of all things and the conjunction of life and death—which, as we know from the illustrations in the *Codex Borgia*, were themes of inexhaustible concern in native religious thought. To the same late period belongs an incense-burner from Cuicuilco in the form of a statuette representing the god of fire or a divinity of the wind and the mountains. It is significant that all these objects with a probable religious content belong to the final phase of the pre-classic period, when no doubt the early stages of the urban revolution were accompanied by a corresponding intellectual ferment.

It is clear, in any event, that at La Venta, and later in the Maya and Zapotec cultures and at Teotihuacán, the arts of sculpture, of painting, of engraving and of pottery reflect an essentially religious mentality. We are totally ignorant of Olmec religion, which seems—if we may judge from the carvings and engravings on jade—to have been centred on the cult of a jaguar god and a child, a "baby" with features which in varying degrees resemble those of a feline. At Teotihuacán the principal deities are the god of rain and of vegetation, later to bear the Nahuatl name of Tlaloc *(Plate 39)*, and the Feathered Serpent, the symbol of the mysterious forces of the earth. The face of the same rain god, known to the Mayas as Chac and to the Zapotecs as Cocijo *(Plates 91, 99)*, appears innumerable times on the façades of the Maya palaces of Yucatán and on the funerary urns of

Monte Albán. Among the southern Mayas the predominant divinities are the serpent gods of Yaxchilán and the maize gods of Palenque.

It must be recorded that there are also a number of carvings or frescoes on secular themes, for example at Piedras Negras and Bonampak. But, in general, sacred art is of infinitely greater importance in the cities than any other. At Teotihuacán, apart from a few pictures of everyday life on vases (for example, a scene of hunting with the blow-gun on a fragment of pottery in the Musée de l'Homme, Paris), all the carvings and frescoes we have are on religious themes—representations of divinities and of priests, ritual scenes, and pictures of the supernatural world and the life beyond. It was perhaps at Teotihuacán that theocracy attained its most absolute form, for not a single carving or painting found here seems to contain any reference to a civil or military leader or a historical event. Some stelae at Monte Albán can be interpreted as referring to events such as the conquest of particular places, but the immense majority of works of plastic art are on religious themes.

Classic Maya art achieved such mastery and such variety that the range of subjects here is wider than elsewhere. The Bonampak frescoes give detailed pictures of court life in a small Maya princedom of the 7th century, and of fighting and dancing. The stelae of Piedras Negras show high dignitaries being presented with captives bound hand and foot; and some of the Palenque carvings deal with historical events. Finally at Lubaantún in British Honduras and in particular on the island of Jaina off Campeche there developed an individual art style of extraordinary vitality and charm, producing painted terracotta figurines which represent a great range of human types in their characteristic dress and ornaments and in all the postures of everyday life *(Plates 74–81, 83, 84, 87)*.

But, having said this, we must agree that the majority of the carvings, statues and inscriptions are concerned with religion, from the scenes of self-mortification on the lintels at Yaxchilán to the magnificent wall panels in the Temples of the Sun and of the Cross at Palenque. And if we consider the pottery we do certainly find some vases with pictures of everyday life or representations of plants or animals, but many others are moulded or painted in the image of supernatural beings: for example the splendid orange-coloured vase decorated with the face of the sun god which was found at Palenque.

If we ventured, on the flimsy basis of our existing knowledge, to compare the two most important classic civilisations, the people of Teotihuacán and the Mayas, we might perhaps say that the former civilisation was more theocratic, and consequently less military, than the latter. The art of Teotihuacán contains no representation of a warrior or an armed man (with one exception in which a man is shown carrying javelins with a rounded end instead of a point), and no battle scenes. The Mayas seem to have been a fairly peaceable people, but the Bonampak frescoes and a number of the Piedras Negras stelae show quite clearly that in addition to priests they also had military commanders who led the warriors into battle and enjoyed the honours of victory. There must thus have been a double hierarchy of authority in the Maya cities, whereas on the high plateau all power was in the hands of the priests.

However this may be, the prevailing tendency for nearly a thousand years was, in general, the dominance of a priestly class whose members possessed a monopoly of writing, of astronomy and of divination, determined the most propitious dates for work in the fields, conducted ceremonies, and planned and organised the execution of building work and sculpture. These priests were probably identified with the gods themselves, as was the case in a later period, and in consequence enjoyed immense veneration and exercised immense power among the peasant masses.

To this intellectual class must be attributed the series of great inventions which marked the transition from village to town—monumental architecture, the art of writing, the calendar. There is no evidence that human sacrifice was ever practised at Teotihuacán or Monte Albán, and in Maya territory there are only occasional traces of the practice. The classical portrait of the priest-king Quetzalcoatl, the Feathered Serpent, as he was traditionally depicted in the Aztec period—the figure of a wise ruler, kindly and virtuous, opposed to warfare and human sacrifice, the inventor of writing and all the arts—is an idealised portrait of the theocracy of Teotihuacán.

Decline and Revival

This theocratic civilisation, the golden age of the native civilisations of Mexico, came to an end between the 9th and the 11th century, at different times in different areas—earlier at Teotihuacán, later at Monte Albán.

Archaeology has revealed a number of features which show evidence of this decline: the slowing down and then the cessation of new building and carving, the abandonment of the Maya practice of erecting dated stelae, the disappearance of the pottery types characteristic of the classic period. Sometimes there is evidence of the intrusion of peoples of other races—for example at Palenque, where a wing of the Palace was occupied by an immigrant people from the Coast who brought with them their characteristic stone "yokes". But of the causes and the nature of this displacement of the great classic civilisations we know nothing.

It would probably be an error to think of the end of this period as a sudden violent cataclysm. Only exceptionally do we find signs of deliberate destruction. The picture is rather that of a gradual abandonment of the large cities and a return to rural life in the scattered villages.

There are, of course, considerable differences from area to area. Among the southern Mayas, in the very cradle of Maya civilisation, the erection of stelae ceases not later than the end of the 9th century, and the towns seem to have been rapidly and completely abandoned. In the favourable climate of this area the jungle must very soon have reclaimed the land deserted by man and swallowed up the buildings, leaving only a few peasants cultivating their maize like the few score Lacandone Indians who still eke out a living in the forests of this region. We have no inkling of the fate of the ruling classes, the priests and the warriors. Did the Maya aristocracy perish in battle—though it must be admitted that we have no evidence of any conflict? Did they migrate to Yucatán? The latter theory seems more likely, at any rate so far as some of the priests and leaders are concerned. Others may have reverted to the life of their ancestors and become ordinary peasants.

In Oaxaca the ceremonial centre of Monte Albán was abandoned by the Zapotecs, who throughout the following centuries were continually being driven farther back by their mountain neighbours, the Mixtecs. The Mixtecs took over their buildings and palaces and even their tombs, unceremoniously clearing out the bodies to make room for their own dead. Tomb No. 7, for example, was found by Alfonso Caso to contain an extraordinary wealth of Mixtec gold jewellery and engraving within a burial chamber which was clearly Zapotec. We find the same thing at Mitla, where the Mixtecs decorated the walls built by their precedessors with paintings based on their own religious and cosmological conceptions.

As for the civilisation of Teotihuacán, it appears that after the dispersal of the inhabitants of the great city some of them founded a colony at Azcapotzalco, near the lagoon of Mexico, where their culture survived for two centuries. It is probable that the aristocracy of Teotihuacán, a relatively small group of the population, came from the tropical lands of the Gulf Coast to the east, and had achieved dominance over farming peoples like the untutored Otomi tribe. The priestly class of Teotihuacán thus did not have to go far afield to find a new home, taking with them the greater part of the knowledge and traditions of which they were the repository, and which in due course were to awaken to fresh life.

What, then, was the cause of the decline which overtook all the classic civilisations, though in different ways? A great variety of explanations have been suggested. It has been noted in our own day that in these areas of tropical vegetation the farming technique known as *milpa* agriculture rapidly exhausts the soil and obliges the farmer to seek fresh land every three to five years, since the yield of cereals progressively falls and the scrub rapidly overruns his fields. Then he must move on, clear another patch of forest, and fertilise the soil with wood ash. It is suggested that techniques of this kind, which are appropriate to a scattered rural population, must have proved inadequate to provide food supplies for the towns, and that the classic Maya civilisation collapsed for want of a proper economic basis.

This theory fits in reasonably well with the observed facts in the tropical regions, but not with the agriculture of the high plateau, where the problems are quite different. In this area it was drought that was the enemy, as is shown by the importance attributed to the cult of the rain god. But so long as there was enough rain and proper irrigation the central plains and valleys were reasonably fertile.

There is certainly something in the "economic" theory. It is true that the native pattern of agriculture founded on maize and a few other plants, without any stock rearing, was adequate to supply village communities but was unable to meet the needs of towns of any size, particularly with a large ruling class which did not work on the land. Moreover—and this is true of the Mayas, of Teotihuacán, and of Oaxaca—the aristocracy of the towns must have imposed a crushing burden on their subjects in the building of their gigantic monuments with no other source of energy than man's unaided muscles. Lacking animals and vehicles, and so far as we know without winches or pulleys, the builders had to rely on the labour of men's own hands to transport enormous monoliths, to pile up hundreds of thousands of tons of earth, to erect pyramids and palaces, staircases, terraces and platforms. Moreover the countless sculptors, painters, engravers and potters whose work has come down to us would have to be provided with subsistence by the community. Thus a considerable part of the peasants' output went into the production of buildings and works of art, the outstanding quality of which we can admire today, but which nevertheless must have been a heavy burden on the shoulders of the Indian farmers.

And finally, although the religions of the classic period preserved for almost a thousand years a basically agricultural character which would appeal to a rural population, we may reasonably suspect that the metaphysical speculations of the priests would increasingly tend to soar above the practical and down-to-earth religion to which the villagers remained attached. Even today the Indians of the country areas, Christians as they now are, have their own ways of practising their adopted religion, and as a rule are little concerned with orthodoxy or with dogma. In the classic Maya peoples it may well be that the peculiar importance which the priests attached to the observation of heavenly bodies and to chronological computations took them progressively farther away from the simple country rites which appealed to the peasant masses as a means of ensuring bountiful harvests; and these same peasants could see little utility in remote and incomprehensible calculations covering some millions of years.

Since it is likely that the priests of Copán or Teotihuacán jealously maintained the secret of their writing system and their abstruse speculations—it is significant that some Maya inscriptions contain errors clearly due to the fact that the carver was trying to reproduce symbols which he did not understand—we may suppose that an ever deeper gulf would develop between them and the mass of the peasants. And, having once lost their influence in spiritual matters, the rulers could not impose their authority by the coercive methods which the Aztecs later successfully applied. The divorce between town and country was now complete, and urban life, lacking the supplies and the labour force which only the villages could provide, inevitably decayed.

On this theory, therefore, the decline of all the classic civilisations of ancient Mexico was due to the disproportion between the effort required for their support and the resources available, and in particular to the turning away of the country people from the priestly class, at varying pace and on a varying scale in different areas. The urban revolution was thus brought to an end by another revolution in which the towns paid the penalty for their earlier treatment of the villages.

One cycle was thus completed; and a new one now began when a people of incomers settled on the central plateau. These were the Toltecs, who founded Tollan (Tula), the "place of reeds", on the site of an Otomi township called Mamêhni in the middle of the 9th century—in the year *cetecpatl* (1 Flint), or 856 of our era, according to the traditional account.

Unlike the founders of Teotihuacán, the Toltecs came from the north; in all probability they spoke a dialect of the great Uto-Aztec language family. This was the first appearance on the stage of history of the Nahuatl-speaking Indians who were henceforth to dominate the whole Mexican cultural scene.

The Toltec period lasted some three centuries (856 to 1168). The written sources are numerous and detailed. Both Sahagún's Aztec informants and the chroniclers like Ixtlilxochitl who used ancient texts give us full accounts of the history of the Toltecs and descriptions of their life. The problem which faces the modern student is to determine how these tales, semi-historical and semi-mythical, are to be reconciled with the findings of archaeology.

Clearly, for example, we cannot accept that most of the Toltec rulers reigned for exactly 52 years, the length of a cycle in their chronology; but this does not mean that the lists of kings are necessarily false, or that the events described have no basis in reality. Near the Tula excavations is a rock on which are carved a feathered serpent, a face which has been intentionally mutilated, and the date *ce-acatl* (1 Reed); and this fits in with the tradition that Quetzalcoatl was born in the year 1 Reed, 947, and was driven out of Tula 52 years later, i.e., also in the year 1 Reed.

The ruins of Tula partly confirm the tradition about the Toltecs *(Plates 132, 133, 135)*. One proof is provided by the large scale on which the theme of the Feathered Serpent is used in the sculpture and the architecture. But the friezes of tigers and jaguars are in complete contradiction with the same tradition, which said that Quetzalcoatl induced the Toltecs to abandon the practice of human sacrifice.

The whole body of historical or legendary tales and epic poems relating to Tula suggests, when interpreted in the light of the archaeological evidence, that there were three successive cultural phases in the life of the city. During the first phase, which lasted rather more than a century, the Nahuatl-speaking Toltec incomers took over the main structures and theocratic ideas of the great towns of the classic civilisations, which still survived at Azcapotzalco, Chalco and Xochicalco. At Azcapotzalco a "late Teotihuacán" stage still persisted. Xochicalco, on the western slope of the plateau, was an active centre in which—to judge from the style of the carvings and the chronological hieroglyphs on the pyramid—there was a mingling of influences from Teotihuacán, the Zapotecs and even the Mayas. Chalco served as a link or staging point between the Valley of Mexico and the lower-lying warmer areas. The Toltec civilisation was born of a synthesis, and it is likely enough that in its early stages this synthesis was the work of a ruling class which grew out of the old priestly aristocracy. This would explain some features recorded in the traditions. Thus

Quetzalcoatl and his adepts were said to speak a language of their own; the Toltec religion was based on the cult of the primal couple (the god of fire and the goddess of the earth) and on the worship of the rain god Tlaloc *(Plate 39)* who, according to the native historian Ixtlilxochitl, had been worshipped in a remote and fabulous past by giants (that is, by the pre-Toltec inhabitants of central Mexico); and human sacrifice was forbidden. All this would suggest that during this first phase the Toltecs were prepared, whether voluntarily or not, to accept the leadership of a minority of Teotihuacán origin who were much ahead of them in intellectual achievement.

The second phase (covering the second half of the 10th century) was wholly taken up with a long series of conflicts and public calamities—civil wars, pestilences, famine, and destruction of all kinds—which the traditional tales present in summary and dramatic form as a rivalry between Tezcatlipoca, the sorcerer god of the night sky and the Great Bear, and Quetzalcoatl, the priest-king of Tula. This Quetzalcoatl, whose name signifies literally "serpent (decorated with) *quetzal* plumes", is also designated by the date of his birth, *ce-acatl*, "1 Reed", and by the title of *Topiltzin*, "our revered ruler". He is both a divine personage, the Feathered Serpent, the great earth god of Teotihuacán, and a historical person who lived between 950 and 1000 and was the last priest-king of Tula and the leader of a priestly and conservative party. Tezcatlipoca *(Plates 157, 158, 169)*, on the other hand, symbolises the astral gods of the warlike tribes and the revolutionary drive of the immigrant peoples. The conflict between these two was the struggle between the religious, social and political conceptions belonging to the classic traditions and the ideas of the incomers.

It may well be that this conflict was initiated by the arrival of large groups of incomers from other Nahua tribes, represented by the astral god Tezcatlipoca. The victory of this new god over Quetzalcoatl compelled the priest-king to flee; and this marked the beginning of the third phase, which was to last—according to the traditional dates—from 999 to 1168.

On the hypothesis just stated, this third phase corresponds to the Toltec civilisation proper, as it existed after breaking free from the influence of Teotihuacán. Architecture now achieved a flexibility unknown on the central plateau, combining pyramids and colonnades to create an entirely new style. Large halls were built for assemblies of warriors, the new military aristocracy. The sanctuaries were now larger: they were no longer the preserve of a small number of priests, jealous of their prerogatives, but were thrown open to all. The Feathered Serpent was still an important divinity, but was now included in the Nahuatl pantheon alongside the divinities of the stars and the sun, becoming the god of the Morning Star. Savage and bloody cults became preponderant, and human sacrifice was practised on a large scale. The warriors and their leader, the "king", now enjoyed greater authority than the priests.

Thus Tula in its original form prefigures the cities of the late post-classic phase, and Mexico City in particular. It is interesting to note that even when the Aztecs, in order to satisfy Tezcatlipoca and the great sun god Uitzilopochtli, were becoming ever more deeply involved in the practice of the "flowery war" (sacred war) and of human sacrifice, they still felt a kind of nostalgia for the Toltec golden age when the beneficent Quetzalcoatl had sacrificed only snakes and butterflies. The dualism between the settled farmers and the incomers with their taste for hunting and war, between the theocracy and the military autocracy, between the gods of the fields and the gods of the sky, was to be reflected to the end in the ideas and structures of Mexican civilisation.

One of the consequences of the time of troubles in the 10th century was the spread of groups of Toltecs into other areas. All civil wars lead to movements of peoples; and it was refugees from Tula who joined with a Maya tribe, the Itzá, under the leadership of a personage known as the "Feathered Serpent", to invade Yucatán towards the end of the 10th century and found, on the site of a town of the classic civilisation, a city which they called Chichén Itzá.

149

150

151

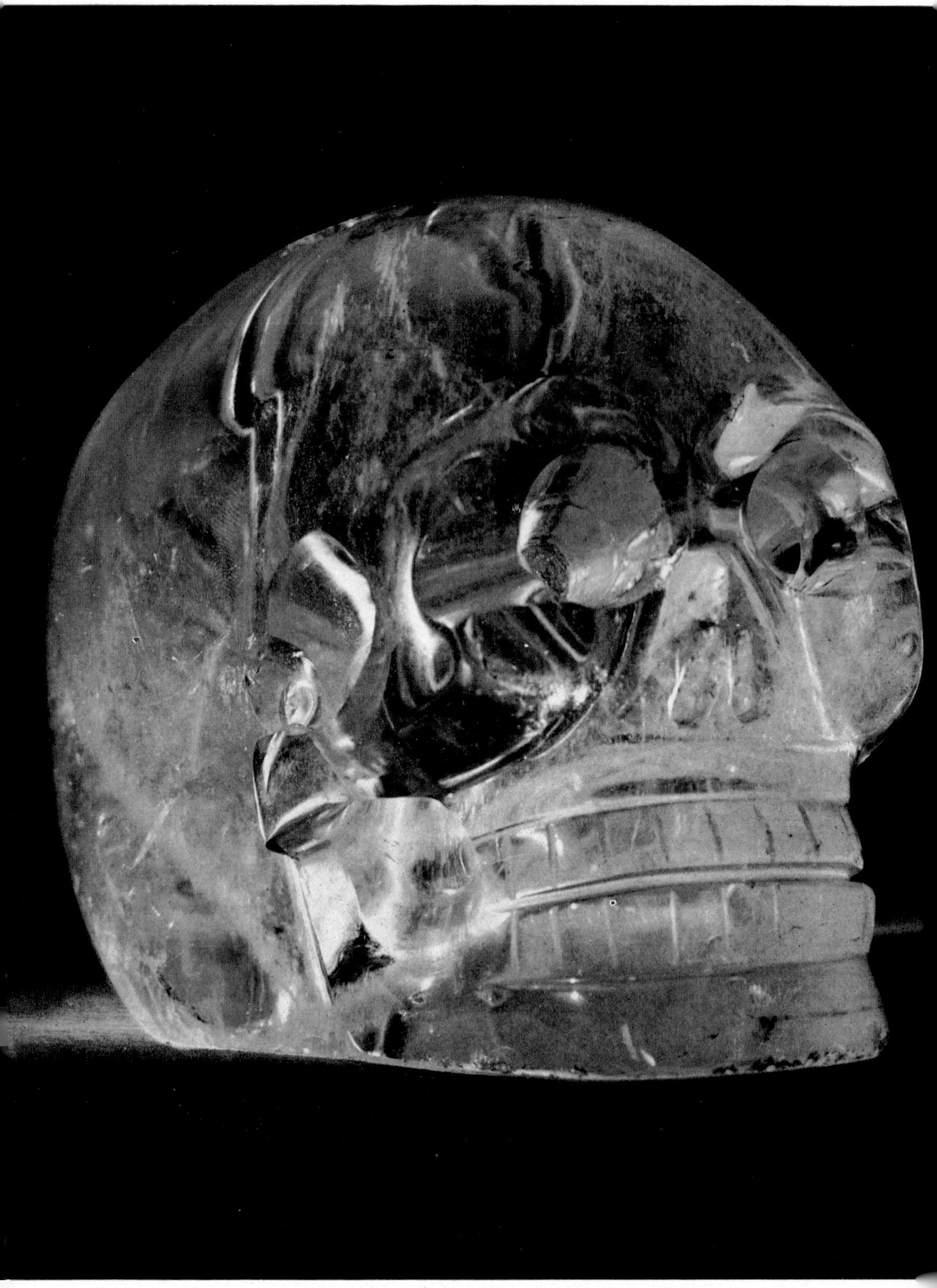

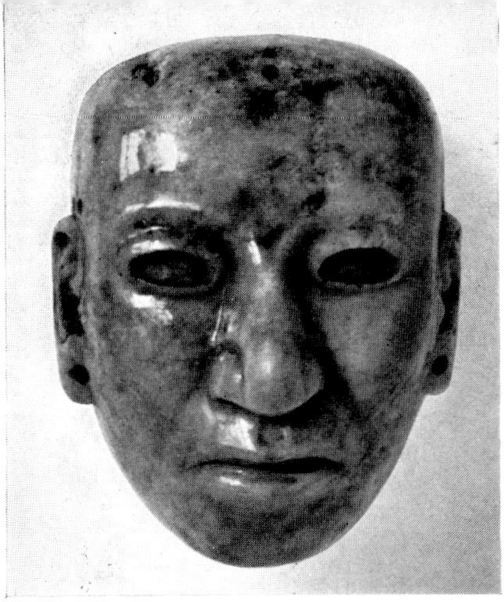

153

154

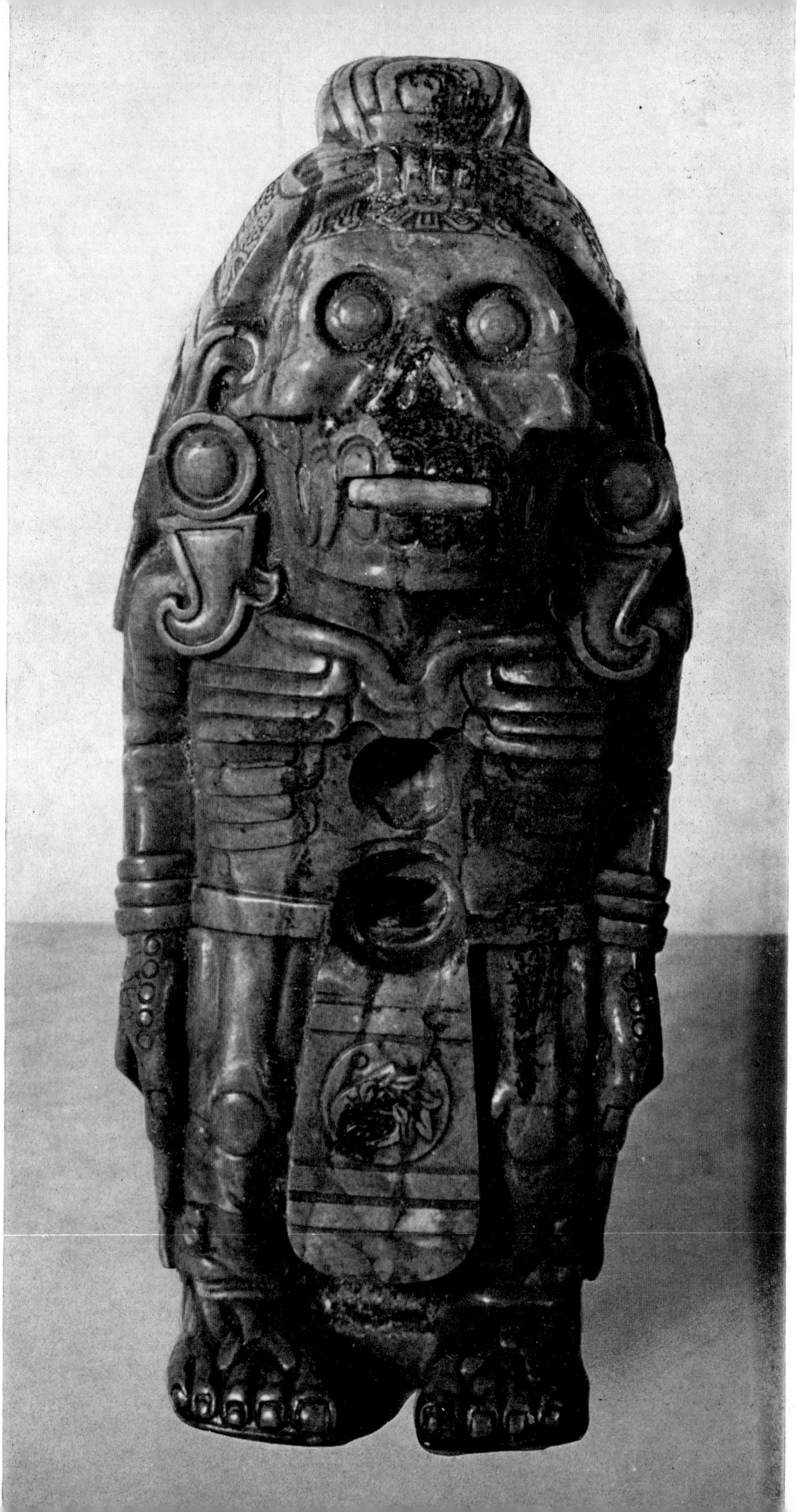

155

156

158

157

There are still many obscurities about the exact dates and sequence of these events, about the Itzá personage known under the name of Quetzalcoatl, and about the origin and characteristics of the Itzá themselves. If the priest-king Quetzalcoatl did indeed leave Tula at the traditional date of 999, how is this to be reconciled with the Maya dates for the arrival of Quetzalcoatl in Yucatán, that is, between 967 and 987? How are we to explain the transformation of the peaceable Feathered Serpent of Tula into the conqueror who came to Yucatán, established the practice of human sacrifice and was worshipped as the god of the Morning Star? Who were the Itzá and where did they come from? (In relation to this latter question it may be significant that some of them at least bore Nahuatl names).

To these questions, and to many others, we are not yet able to offer any answer. What we can say, on the basis of the archaeological evidence, is that the architecture of Chichén Itzá is identical in all respects to the architecture of Tula, whereas the sculpture shows a mingling of typically Maya themes like the figure of the rain god Chac and Toltec themes like the feathered serpent. And there are some gold discs—the gold was imported from Central America and wrought locally—engraved with scenes of Toltec inspiration such as sacrifices or fights, but showing a refinement and delicacy of workmanship which betrays the hand of a Maya craftsman.

With their large colonnaded halls, their square pillars carved with figures of heavily armed warriors, their sanctuaries approached by gateways supported by feathered serpents, their staircases with the figures of standard-bearers, their ritual statues of recumbent figures known as *chacmools*, the great buildings of Tula and Chichén Itzá show such striking resemblances that the common origin of the two styles is manifest *(Plates 125, 126, 130–133, 135)*.

The Toltec revival on the central plateau ended, according to the traditional account, in 1168. It is significant that a systematic attempt was made to destroy the Temple of the Morning Star at Tula: a ramp was built against one side of the pyramid so that the destroyers could roll down the caryatids in the form of warriors which supported the roof of the sanctuary. Probably the fall of the city was due both to internal dissension and to invasion. After the abandonment of Tula substantial Toltec settlements remained in certain areas on the central plateau, particularly at Cholula, a cult centre and place of pilgrimage in honour of Quetzalcoatl, at Chapultepec and above all at Colhuacán, which, two centuries later, was to hand on the torch to the Aztecs.

In Yucatán the Toltec-Maya revival lasted until the beginning of the 13th century. In the following centuries, during a period of Mayapán dominance followed by a succession of wars between petty states, the Maya civilisation entered a phase of complete decadence which continued until the arrival of the Conquistadors. Here again archaeology confirms the evidence of history and tradition. Mayapán, with its impressive walls but its poorly constructed buildings and its total lack of any plastic art, reflects the distresses of a time when there was no respite from continual conflict and the only surviving architecture was the architecture of fortifications.

The Toltec civilisation also exerted considerable influence, during its period of flowering and even after this, outside the main Toltec area of Tula and the Toltec-Maya area in Yucatán. The excavations and the study of pottery, statuary and wall paintings have made it possible to identify specifically Toltec themes (*chacmools*, processions of personages with splendid plumes on their heads, geometric decoration of pottery, and so on), not only on the central plateau but along the Gulf Coast from the mouth of the Pánuco to the Tabasco, in Huaxtec and Totonac territory; to the west, among the Tarascans of Michoacán; on the borders of the Cholula and Tlaxcala plateau, reaching right into the mountains of Oaxaca, where the Toltec tradition fused with the art of the Mixtecs to produce a particularly successful synthesis. Still farther away, in Guatemala, the Maya-speaking

Quiche Indians incorporated in their cosmological myths and their tribal legends themes borrowed from the Toltecs and expressed in words of Nahuatl origin.

Although we no longer share the illusions of the 16th century Mexicans or the older authors about the remote antiquity of Toltec civilisation or its status as the mother civilisation of Mexico, we are bound to note that the body of evidence gathered by archaeology rather tends to confirm these traditions. It enables us to assert, at any rate, that the central focus of this civilisation was in fact at Tula, that it did in fact establish itself in Yucatán, and that it spread widely beyond its original starting point.

The Formation of the Post-Toltec States

For the period following the collapse of Tula we have a series of valuable native documents, consisting of illustrated and pictographic manuscripts like the *Codex Xolotl* and the *Tlotzin* and *Quinatzin* "Mapas". In these works, which after the Spanish conquest provided essential material for the chroniclers and particularly for Ixtlilxochitl, we can follow, generation by generation, the arrival of new tribes in central Mexico, the various stages of their establishment, and the foundation of the various towns and dynasties.

According to the *Codex Xolotl*, tribes of hunters in the north, "barbarians" who probably spoke non-Toltec dialects of the Nahuatl language family, learned in 1168 that Tula had been destroyed. They then advanced southward, penetrated into the central valleys from the ruins of Tula to the great lagoon without striking a blow, and took possession of the country. Their leader was called Xolotl *(Plates 155–156)*, a semi-legendary figure who was supposed to have ruled for more than a hundred years. His name is that of a minor but important god in the body of myth about Quetzalcoatl, who after the disappearance of the god of the Morning Star descended into the underworld of Mictlan and brought back the bones of the dead so that he might breathe fresh life into them. Accordingly he was represented with the head of a dog, for dogs were sacrificed so that they might accompany the dead on their journey into the underworld. The symbolism is quite clear: Quetzalcoatl (the Toltec civilisation) has disappeared, but Xolotl comes from the north (Mictlan, the abode of the dead) to give new life to this civilisation. Here again we find the typical Mexican tendency to fit a particular series of events both into historical reality and into the world of myth.

Xolotl—by which we are probably to understand a succession of leaders of northern tribes—now settled on the central plateau. It is significant that all the places where he halted have names and hieroglyphs containing the word *oztotl*, meaning "cave". These *Chichimeca* of the early 13th century built no houses, had no clothing but skins, and hunted with the bow and arrow. But from the start they established relations, sometimes friendly and sometimes hostile, with the small Toltec towns which still survived, and in particular with Colhuacán, situated on a peninsula on the edge of the lagoon. According to the *Codex Xolotl* the son of the barbarian conqueror, Nopaltzin, married the daughter of the "king" of Colhuacán—though this did not prevent him from making war on the town. What is clear, however, is that the incomers very soon began to learn from the Toltecs. According to the native documents, they adopted a settled mode of life as farmers at the end of the 13th century; in the 14th century their ruler Quinatzin, whose capital was at Texcoco on the eastern shore of the lake, brought from the Mixtec mountains a tribe descended from Toltec refugees in order that his town might possess the arts of goldsmithing and illumination; and his successor, who had been brought up by a woman of noble family in Colhuacán, made the use of the Toltec language (i.e., the Nahuatl language of Tula) compulsory and replaced the simple religion of his ancestors by the complex ritual and the crowded pantheon of the ancient cities.

Towards the end of the 14th century at latest all the *Chichimeca*, apart from a handful of inveterate hunters who preferred to seek refuge in the mountains and lead a free and wandering life rather than cultivate the soil, had settled down to a sedentary existence and had taken over the substance of Toltec civilisation in the late forms found at Colhuacán, Cholula and elsewhere.

The evidence of archaeology suggests not only that the native accounts were accurate, but also perhaps that the cultural evolution of the immigrants proceeded even more rapidly than the native manuscripts indicate. The pyramid of Tenayuca, formed as it is of a series of superimposed structures, was begun in the early part of the 13th century, no doubt on the occasion of the New Fire of 1247; that is, barely a generation after the arrival of "Xolotl" on the central plateau. The invaders seem to have settled first at Tenayuca; and, though still living in caves, they set out to build a sanctuary after the model of the Toltecs, and probably under their technical direction.

The pottery of the Valley of Mexico also yields valuable evidence. The newcomers were nomadic hunters who were ignorant of the use of pottery; but here again they adopted Toltec practices. Toltec pottery, characterised by vases of simple shapes with geometric decoration—very different from the pottery of Teotihuacán and much less refined—is the source of the pottery found at Tenayuca and all over the Valley of Mexico until the Aztec period.

The Toltec refugees on the Cholula plateau came into contact with the Mixtecs and created a new type of pottery, decorated with mythological themes and painted in polychrome, of striking richness and decorative effect. This splendid pottery, which achieved a well-deserved reputation as a luxury product, began to be imported into the Valley of Mexico in the 14th century for the use of chiefs and high dignitaries of the tribes who had earlier been regarded as barbarians.

Thus in the 13th and 14th centuries there co-existed on the central plateau a late Toltec or "epigonal" phase in towns like Colhuacán, Xochimilco, Chapultepec and Cholula, and a "formative" phase of the new city states which were then being established in considerable numbers. The *Chichimeca* who had come with Xolotl were followed by other Nahuatl-speaking tribes, like the one which founded Tlaxcala. The *Tepaneca* ("those who live on the stone", that is, on the lava flow from the volcano of Xitle)—who were not, perhaps, originally a Nahua people but may have been related to the Otomi—occupied Azcapotzalco and became involved in a series of wars and acts of violence in order to impose their dominance over the whole plateau. The Otomi, following the general trend, founded a small state of their own at Xaltocan.

The *Relaciones* of Ixtlilxochitl refer to twenty-eight states as existing in the 14th century, the most important of these being Texcoco (the descendants of Xolotl), Azcapotzalco (the *Tepaneca*), Tlaxcala and Huexotzinco. Like the Greek cities of the ancient world, and probably also like the classic Maya cities, each of these states consisted of a town built round the temple of the tribal divinity and of the surrounding countryside. Trading relations grew up between the various states, and their ruling dynasties were linked to one another by marriage—though, in spite of this, war was almost endemic between the states, as each of them tried by force or by cunning to achieve dominance over as many as possible of the others and compel them to pay tribute.

Each of these cities was governed by a chief, who was generally elected—the machinery of election differing from state to state—and came from a particular family. This was the *Tlatoani*, "he who speaks". He was usually assisted by various military or civil dignitaries, and by a Great Council or a number of separate Councils: at Texcoco, for example, there were four Councils, one for government and justice, one for music and learning, one for war, and one for finance. The priests, who were important and respected, had access to the Councils but did not govern, except at Cholula where the high priest of the Feathered Serpent wielded power in accordance with the tradition of Teotihuacán and the first phase at Tula.

During these two centuries all the new cities underwent an intense process of "Toltecisation". When the ruler of Texcoco was killed in 1418 at the behest of his ambitious neighbour the king of Azcapotzalco his body was burned in accordance with Toltec rites. It is fair to say that at this period all the heterogeneous features imported by various invaders were fused together, that the Nahuatl language was known and used everywhere, at least for purposes of communication, and that—apart from the tribal cults peculiar to each city—there was a common body of religious beliefs and rituals. The political fragmentation of the country was counterbalanced by a marked cultural unity.

In this area, in contrast to developments in Yucatán at the same period, the instability of the states and their continual internecine struggles do not seem to have led to a fall in the intellectual and artistic level. The warring states were still very receptive to outside influences. Their warriors, and to an even greater extent their merchants, undertook long journeys to distant parts. From the Tula period onwards there is evidence of connections between the central plateau and the Huaxtec region on the Gulf Coast, on the one hand, and the Pacific slope of the mountains on the other. Gold and copper working and the cult of Xipe Totec *(Plates 141, 162)*, the golddsmith's god, were imported from the Mixtec-Zapotec area. A study of the native manuscripts of the Mixtec region *(Codex Nuttall) (Plates 137–139)* and of the area between Cholula and Oaxaca *(Codex Borgia)* reveals very striking similarities. If we compare the subject matter and the styles illustrated in these works with the pottery of the Mixtecs and of Cholula, with the Mitla wall paintings and the frescoes on the altar at Tizatlán, we can see that the greater part of the present state of Puebla, the state of Tlaxcala and the Mixtec country in Oaxaca formed a cultural area of substantial homogeneity from the point of view of art, mythology and chronology. Elements of Toltec origin, post-Toltec Nahua elements and Mixtec elements were associated in the "Mixteca-Puebla" style which had a considerable influence on Aztec art *(Plates 137–140, 143, 145–148)*.

it appears, therefore, that at the beginning of the 15th century, when the formative phase of the post-Toltec states was coming to an end, the whole of Mexico between Xilotepec in the north and Mitla in the south formed a single cultural area. No doubt a variety of languages were spoken, but Nahuatl was dominant. No doubt there was a great difference between the country-bred Otomi and the Mixtecs, those skilled goldsmiths *(Plate 136)*, but both of them were increasingly being caught up into the Nahua ethnic group and the Nahua civilisation. All these peoples employed the same system of writing and the same chronology, similar to that of the classic Mayas though less complex in pattern and less abstract in appearance; and all of them were continually borrowing rites, customs, gods and styles from one another.

The Aztec Synthesis

The tribe known as the *Mexico* or *Azteca* (so called in memory of the country of Aztlán which they had left in 1168, the date of the fall of Tula, after dwelling there, according to their own traditions, for rather more than a thousand years) were late arrivals in the central valley and, finding all the land occupied, had to establish their "capital" of Tenochtitlán in the marshes of the lagoon. It was not until half a century later, in 1375, that the Aztecs became sufficiently important to appoint a *tlatoani*, who was related to the Toltec dynasty of Colhuacán. This first king and his two immediate successors—in spite of the conquests later attributed to them in the much embellished chronicles of the tribe—were hard put to it to maintain the autonomy of their little state, and had to accept the over-

←159 161→

160

162

163

164

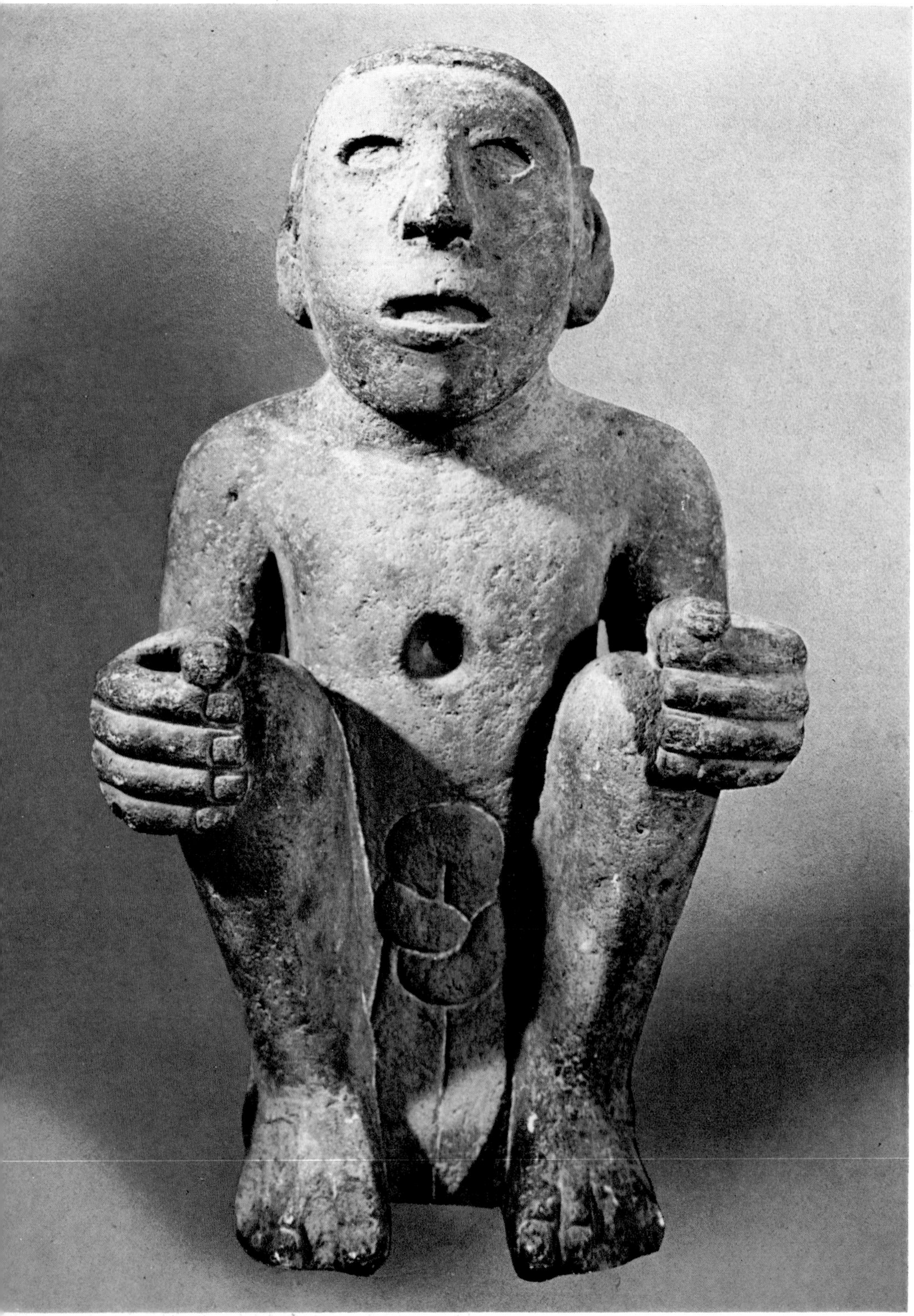

165

166

167

168 →

169

170

171

172

173

174

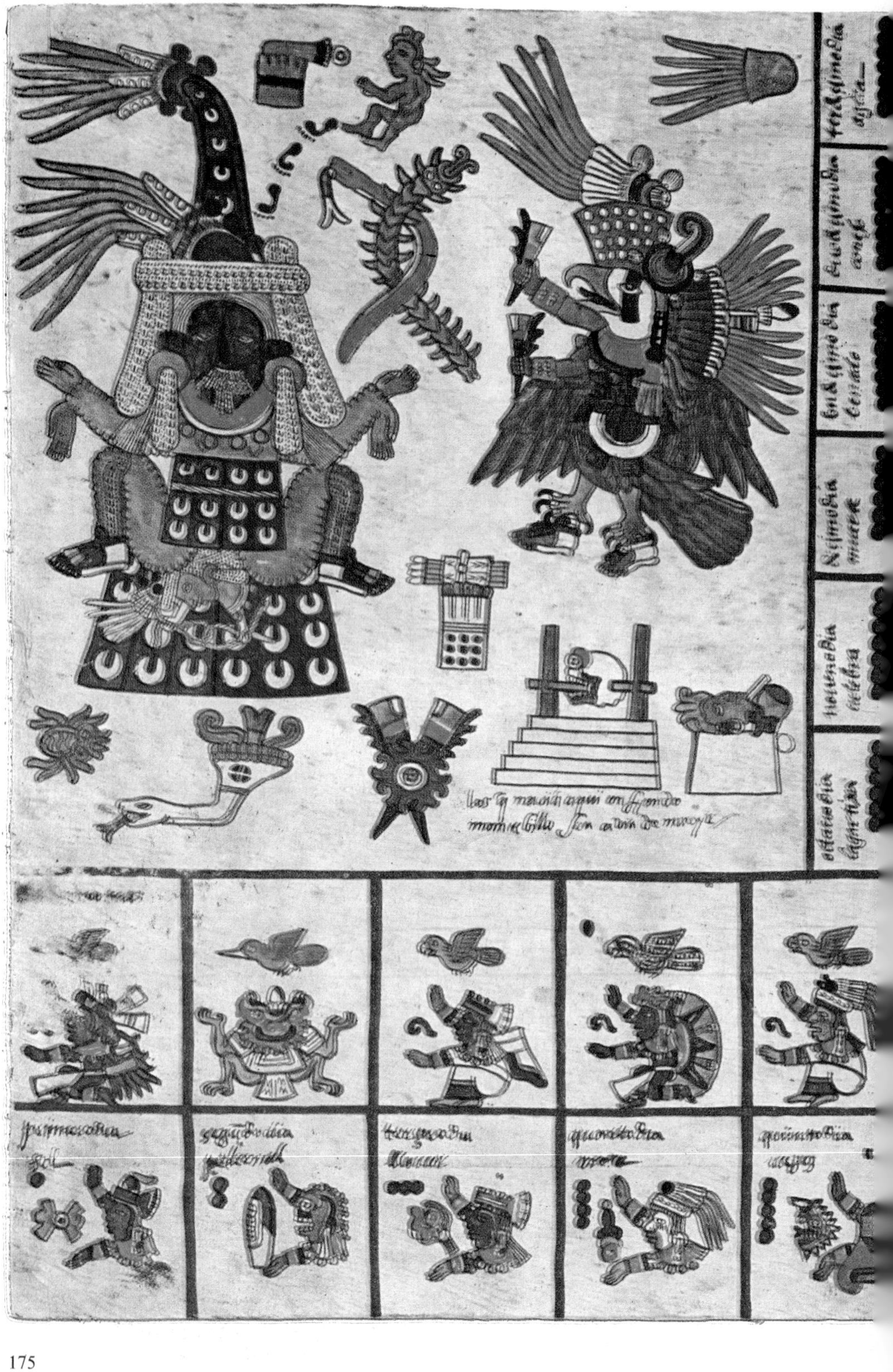

17

177

178

18

181

182

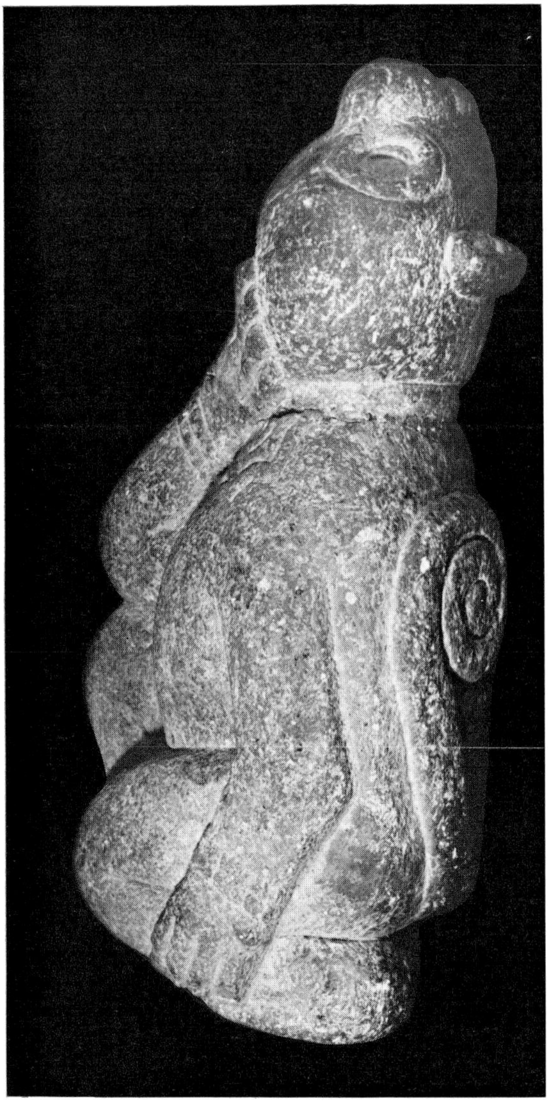

183

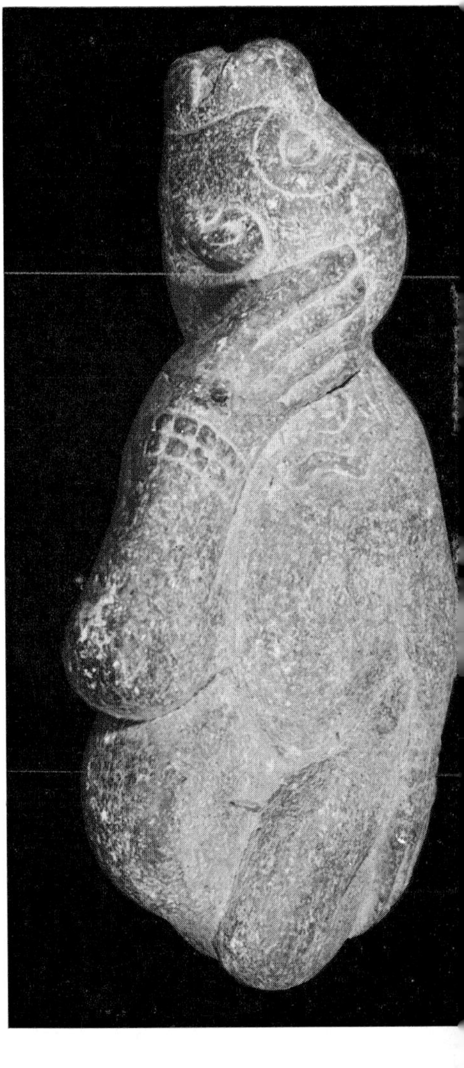

lordship of Colhuacán, and later of Azcapotzalco. The third *tlatoani*, having tried once or twice to demonstrate his independence, was put to death by the *Tepaneca* in 1428.

Nevertheless, in spite of these obscure beginnings, it was the Aztecs who were to undertake the creation of a political unit matching the area of cultural and economic unity. They did not accomplish this task on their own, but as the most dynamic and, at the end of the day, the dominant member of a triple alliance which embraced the city states of Tenochtitlán (Mexico City), Texcoco and Tlacopán. This league of three cities was established in 1429 and lasted until 1521. By the time it fell to a combined attack by the Spaniards and certain native states, including in particular Tlaxcala, the political entity which we call the Aztec empire comprised thirty-eight tributary provinces and stretched from one ocean to the other. A confederation of autonomous cities rather than a centralised state, it contained Nahuatl-speaking peoples along with others who spoke Otomi, Mazahua, Matlaltzinca, Huaxtec, Totonac, Mixtec, Zapotec, Maya and other languages. It did not cover the whole of the Mexican cultural area, for its authority did not extend to Yucatán, nor to Xicalanco (Tabasco-Campeche), Tlaxcala and Metztitlán, the territory of the *Yopi* on the Pacific slope of the plateau, or the kingdom of Michoacán. But it did bring together, under the theoretical authority of the three kings but in fact under that of the Aztec emperor, the main cultural centres of the high plateau, Oaxaca and the Gulf Coast.

The Aztec period is marked by the active development of trade and cultural exchanges, facilitated by the abolition of political barriers. The *pochteca* (merchants) now rose to importance. Thanks to their efforts, and to the work of the collectors of tribute and the military garrisons, the products of the tropical zone flowed in quantity on to the central plateau, which supplied in exchange its own characteristic products. The commonest imports were raw cotton, cotton cloth and articles of dress, feathers and objects made of feathers like helmets, plumes and ceremonial shields, cacao, rubber, jaguar skins, semi-precious stones, gold in the form of dust or bars or discs or jewellery, copper in the form of small flat axes, paper, and certain types of shell, together with maize, oil seeds, beans and timber. Mexico City and the towns on the lagoon exported tools, cloth made of rabbit fur, and pottery.

It is clear, too, that the Aztecs and their neighbours imported not only supplies of goods and manufactured articles but also fashions, rites and ideas. Male and female clothing, hair styles, face painting and tattooing were influenced by the customs of the Otomi or the Totonacs, gold jewellery by Mixtec art, luxury or ritual pottery by the pottery of Cholula. Mexico City, now the busy capital of a large empire, contained a special temple, the *Coacalco*, open to all foreign gods; but on the great *Teocalli* there stood also the twin temples of the rain god Tlaloc, an old country divinity, and the sun god and warrior Uitzilopochtli: the Aztecs had thus contrived to reconcile and associate the two religions, that of the oldest inhabitants of the country and that of the warlike incomers. The Toltec god Quetzalcoatl, the Otomi fire god, the Huaxtec goddess of love and the Yopi god of the goldsmiths also had their worshippers. Certain rites were celebrated by people of other tribes—for example the dance of the Mazatecs, celebrated every eight years in honour of the planet Venus—or accompanied by hymns sung in foreign languages. In short, the whole of Mexican civilisation at this period shows an eclecticism which by no means indicates a decline in powers or a mere aptitude for imitation, and finally reaches its culmination in a masterly synthesis.

Here again the evidence of archaeology coincides with the information we can obtain from the written documents. Aztec architecture took over most of the Toltec themes and forms—pyramids and pillared halls, battlemented walls decorated with snakes' heads, standard-bearers—combining them with other ideas, such as the circular building which was usually dedicated to the god of the winds. We know that there was one of these in Mexico City which was destroyed during the siege of the town; but there is also one at Calixtlahuaca, near Toluca, which is in an excellent state of preservation. Round tumuli are a characteristic feature of the architecture of the Huaxtecs to the north-east, the Totonacs to the east, and the Tarascans to the north-west.

In its extent and the scale of its buildings Mexico City (and no doubt also Texcoco) went far beyond anything that native builders had so far accomplished. The Aztecs may have no architectural innovations to their credit—unless we attribute to them, as some authors are tempted to do, a properly constructed vault still to be seen in the fortress of Oztoman—but they were able to tackle problems which their precedessors had not had to face: the problem of water supply, solved by means of aqueducts, and the problem of access to a town built on a lake, solved by the extraordinary fortified causeways which linked the town with the shores of the lagoon. They were also, so far as we know, the only people to hew out an entire temple, complete with statuary, from the living rock of a mountainside, as they did at the astonishing sanctuary of Malinalco.

Their sculpture shows clearly the influence of the Toltec tradition; but even more evident is the influence of the Nahua-Mixtec art of the Cholula plateau and Oaxaca. This second influence is still more marked in minor arts like mosaic work and the illumination of manuscripts. But here again the Aztec artists and craftsmen did not merely copy the splendid models which lay to hand: they created a style of their own, and put its mark on everything they produced, from colossal monoliths to statuettes.

Although Aztec art is largely dominated by religious conceptions, as the art of the classic civilisations had been, it sometimes managed to break free from this preoccupation with myth and cosmological ideas. Sometimes

—as befits the art of an imperial city—it is concerned to commemorate historical events (the stela recording the foundation of the great *Teocalli*, the Stone of Tizoc); sometimes, returning after many centuries to the naturalistic inspiration of the village potters, it gives graceful expression to the forms and attitudes of human beings, animals or plants.

As their expansion developed the Aztecs naturally erected buildings in the new provinces in accordance with their own conceptions of architecture, like the temples at Huatusco (Veracruz) and Teopanzolco (Morelos). But this diffusion of the Aztec style still left it open to non-Aztec ethnic groups to maintain their own architectural techniques, as we can see from the ruins of Cempoala. In this town, which was contemporary with Mexico City and was under Aztec control, the Totonacs erected buildings in a very individual style considerably different from that of the buildings on the central plateau.

In spite of the abundance of documents and material remains, this late and final period of the native civilisation raises a number of problems which only properly conducted excavations may perhaps enable us to solve. One example may be given. This period is marked by the relative abundance of certain metals: gold is much used for ornament, silver rather less so, copper is used for making axes and various tools, and small T-shaped pieces of copper serve as coins concurrently with cacao beans. We know very little, however, about where the Indians found these metals and the methods of extraction they used. A number of mine workings are known in the valley, but we have no idea what ores were worked here or how they were treated. The origin of the jadeite, nephrite and other semi-precious stones, which the Aztecs regarded much more highly than gold, is equally obscure.

The brilliance of the native civilisations under the dominance of Mexico City must not allow us to forget the other cultural centres which flourished outside the Aztec empire at the same period. The Tarascan kingdom of

Michoacán, covering a very large area which has been very little explored, may be specially mentioned in this connection. A proper archaeologicaf investigation of the territory of the *Yopi* or *Tlappaneca* in the state ol Guerrero would also be of the greatest value, for this area seems to have been the place of origin of a religious, ritual and technical complex which combined skill in goldsmith's work with the proatice of certain types of human sacrifice.

To take another example, we know very little about the late Maya cities on the eastern coast of Yucatán. How, for example, is the Mixtecoid style of the frescoes at Santa Rita Corozal to be explained? What trace was left in the late Maya towns by the incomers from central Mexico—mercenaries or adventurers, mostly of Nahuatl origin, who took an active part in the internal struggles in Yucatán?

At the end of this rapid survey we can appreciate what archaeology has already contributed to our knowledge of Mexican antiquity. It has not only confirmed and amplified the information supplied by the written sources, but has revealed the existence of advanced civilisations and of more backward cultures which existed and developed in remoter times. Our vision of the past has been enlarged and enriched. It has also become more complex, for the provisional picture obtained as a result of the archaeological discoveries itself raises questions the existence of which could not even be suspected a few years ago.

We can at any rate be certain that the hope expressed by the enthusiastic Brasseur de Bourbourg a century ago has now been fulfilled. Given the extent and value of the results achieved by archaeology in the study of the ancient civilisations of Mexico, no one would any longer question the status of Mexican archaeology. It now stands on an equal footing with its seniors, the branches of archaeology concerned with the antiquities of the Old World. Like these other branches of archaeology, and in partnership with them, it is playing its part in throwing fresh light on the long-continued adventure of our species. And indeed are not the different aspects of archaeology, varying according to place and period, so many chapters in a single book whose true subject—comprehended through the works of his hands and of his mind, in his tombs as in his tools, in his hieroglyphs and his statues as in his weapons and his temples—is nothing less than Man himself?

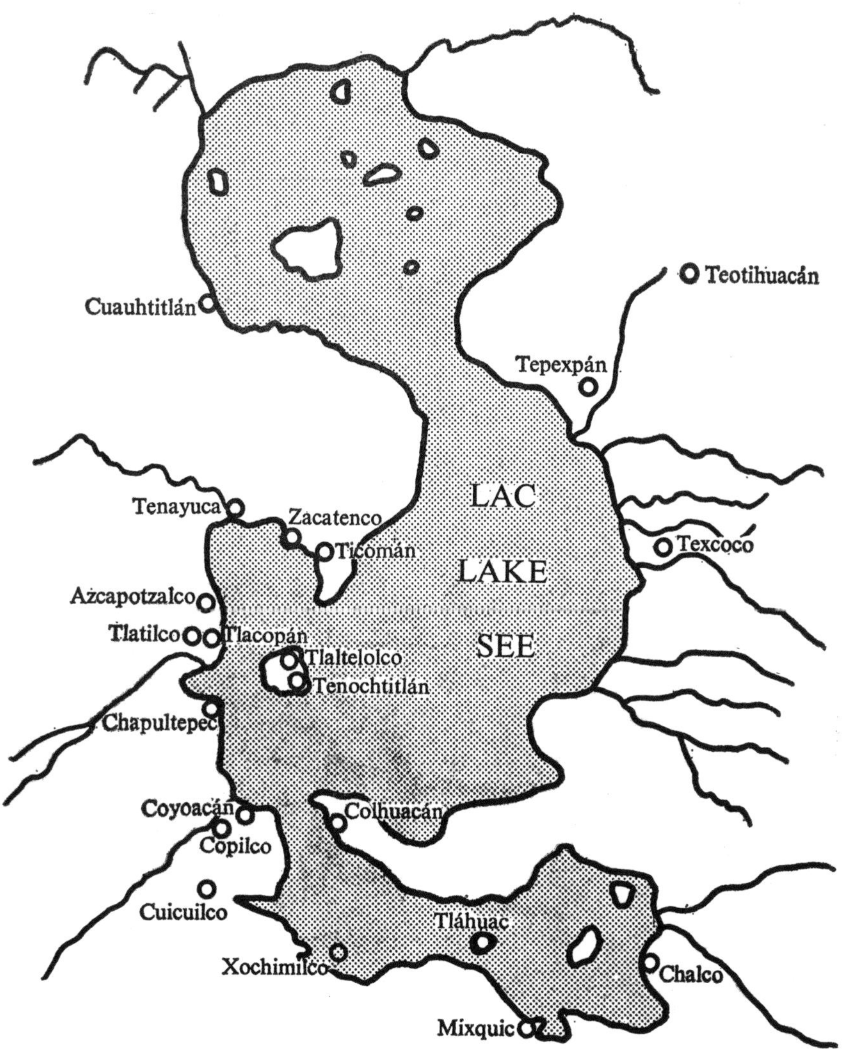

VALLÉE DE MEXICO • VALLEY OF MEXICO

TAL VON MEXIKO

CHRONOLOGICAL TABLE

	North	North-West	Central Plat.	Gulf	Mixteca-Puebla	Oaxaca	Southern Mayas	Northern Mayas
– 20,000	PEOPLES LIVING BY HUNTING AND FOOD–GATHERING							
			Tepexpán					
– 3000	DISCOVERY AND EXPANSION OF AGRICULTURE–NEOLITHIC REVOLUTION–VILLAGES							
– 1500			Zacatenco Copilco Ticomán					
– 300								
– 200				OLMEC FORMATIVE PERIOD				
0		Chupícuaro	Cuicuilco Tlatilco	Olmecs		Monte Albán I and II (0-500)	MAYA FORMATIVE PERIOD	
200	Aztecs at Aztlán ?		Teotihuacán	Apogee of Olmecs ?				
300							292. Date at Tikal Uaxactún	
400			Apogee of Teotihuacán					Oxkintok
500				Late Olmec			MAIN CLASSIC PERIOD	
600		Xochicalco		El Tajín				
700			DECLINE OF TEOT.		692 — Beginning of Mixtec history			
800			Late Teotihuacán					
			856. FOUNDATION OF TULA				889. LAST DATE AT UAXACTÚN	
900			Theocratic phase					

1000			Fall of Quetzalcoatl			DECLINE OF MONTE ALBÁN		TOLTEC-MAYA REVIVAL Chichén Itzá 1000-1200
		Toltec influence at Michoacán	Apogee of Toltecs	Toltec influence at El Tajín and on Huaxtecs	Cholula			
1100					Mixtec expansion towards Oaxaca			
1200	1168. Beginning of migration of Aztecs	Colima, Nayarit, Jalisco: Continuation of pre-classic cultures	1168. FALL OF TULA			Mixtec Invasions		Decline of Mayapán dominance
	Movements of (Nahua) peoples to the south		Arrival Of Xolotla at Tenayuca Formation of states		Tlaxcala	Withdrawal of Zapotecs to Tehuantepec		
1300								
	Chichimeca: Continuation of pre-agricultural way of life		1325 Mexico City	Totonacs	Mixteca-Puebla culture			
1400		Tarascan kingdom Tzintzuntzan	1429. Foundation of League of Three Cities	Cempoala				1450. Fall of Mayapán
1500	AZTEC DOMINANCE							
			1521. Fall of Mexico City					1541. Conquest of Yucatán

SELECT BIBLIOGRAPHY

IGNACIO BERNAL, *Introducción a la arqueología*. Mexico City, 1952.

EUGÈNE BOBAN, *Documents pour servir à l'histoire du Mexique: Catalogue raisonné de la collection de M. Eugène Goupil (ancienne collection J.M.A. Aubin)*. 2 vols, plus atlas. Paris, 1891.

ALFONSO CASO, *El Pueblo del Sol*. Mexico City, 1953.

Codex Borbonicus, ed. E.T. Hamy (facsimile with notes). Paris, 1899.

Codex Borgia, ed. Eduard Seler (facsimile with notes). Mexico City, 1963.

Codex Dresdensis, ed. E. Förstemann. Leipzig, 1880.

Codex Nuttall, ed. Zelia Nuttall. Peabody Museum, Cambridge, Mass., 1902.

MIGUEL COVARRUBIAS, *Indian Art of Mexico and Central America*. New York, 1957.

H.D. DISSELHOFF and J.E.S. LINNÉ, *Ancient America*. "Art of the World", London, 1961.

FERNANDO DE ALVA IXTLILXOCHITL, *Obras Históricas. I: Relaciones. II: Historia Chichimeca*. Mexico City, 1891–2.

WALTER KRICKEBERG, *Altamerikanische Kulturen*. Berlin, 1956.

DIEGO DE LANDA, *Relación de las cosas de Yucatán*, ed. Alfred M. Tozzer. Papers of the Peabody Museum, XVIII. Cambridge, Mass., 1941.

IGNACIO MARQUINA, Arquitectura prehispánica. Mexico City, 1951.

SYLVANUS G. MORLEY, *An introduction to the study of Maya hieroglyphs*. Bureau of American Ethnology, Bulletin 57, Washington, 1915.

SYLVANUS G. MORLEY, *The Ancient Maya*, 3rd ed. (revised by G.W. Brainerd). Stanford, California, and Oxford, 1956.

TATIANA PROSKOURIAKOFF, *A study of classic Maya sculpture*. Publications of the Carnegie Institution of Washington, No. 593, 1950.

PAUL RIVET, *Maya Cities*. London, 1960.

BERNARDINO DE SAHAGÚN, *Historia general de las cosas de Nueva España*, ed. Robredo. Mexico City, 1938.

EDUARD SELER, *Gesammelte Abhandlungen zur amerikanischen Sprach- und Altertumskunde*. Vols I–IV. Berlin, 1902–23.

JACQUES SOUSTELLE, *The Daily Life of the Aztecs on the Eve of the Spanish Conquest*. London, 1961; Penguin Books, 1964.

JACQUES SOUSTELLE, *Arts of Ancient Mexico*. London, 1966.

J. ERIC S. THOMPSON, *Maya hieroglyphic writing—an introduction*. Publications of the Carnegie Institution of Washington, No. 589, 1950; University of Oklahoma Press, 1960 (2nd ed.).

J. ERIC S. THOMPSON, *The Rise and Fall of Maya Civilization*. London, 1956.

GEORGE C. VAILLANT, *Aztecs of Mexico*. Penguin Books, 1965.

LIST OF ILLUSTRATIONS

1 *Pre-classic culture of central plateau (1st millennium B.C.). Steatopygous female figurine. Pottery, hollow, with traces of painting in red. Provenance unknown. Height 36.5 cm; greatest width 15 cm. National Museum of Anthropology, Mexico City. (Ph. U.M. Alama).*

2 *Pre-classic culture of central plateau (1st millennium B.C.). Female figurine. Pottery, hollow, light red glaze, polished. From Tlatilco (Mexico). Height 54.4 cm; width 22.6 cm. National Museum of Anthropology, Mexico City. (Ph. U.M. Alama).*

3 *Pre-classic culture of central plateau (1st millennium B.C.) Pottery jar in truncated cone shape with polished black slip and incised geometric decoration. Provenance unknown. Height 16.5 cm; greatest diameter 16.5 cm. National Museum of Anthropology, Mexico City. (Ph. U.M. Alama).*

4 *The same: another view.*

5 *Pre-classic culture of central plateau (1st millennium B.C.) Bottle-shaped jar in polished black pottery. Incised decoration: stylisation of jaguar's claw. From Tlatilco (Mexico). Height 21 cm; diameter 13 cm. National Museum of Anthropology, Mexico City. (Ph. U.M. Alama).*

6 *Pre-classic culture of central plateau (1st millennium B.C.) Bottle-shaped jar in polished black pottery. Incised decoration: stylisation of jaguar's claw. From Tlatilco (Mexico). Height 22 cm; diameter 14.3 cm. National Museum of Anthropology, Mexico City. (Ph. U.M. Alama).*

7 *Culture of western Mexico (4th-8th centuries?) Pottery figurine of a dog fattened for human consumption. Polished reddish slip. From Colima. Height 13.5 cm; length 31.5 cm. National Museum of Anthropology, Mexico City. (Ph. U.M. Alama).*

8 *Culture of western Mexico (4th-8th centuries?) Statuette representing a hunchback. Pottery. From Ocotlán (Jalisco). Height 23.4 cm. National Museum of Anthropology, Mexico City. (Ph. U.M. Alama).*

9 *Pre-classic culture of central plateau (1st millennium B.C.) Jar in polished black pottery representing a tortoise. From Yautepec (Morelos). Length 17 cm; greatest width 9 cm; height 6.2 cm. National Museum of Anthropology, Mexico City. (Ph. U.M. Alama).*

10–13 *Pre-classic culture of central plateau (1st millennium B.C.) Four female figurines, ranging from 9.5 to 12.7 cm in height. From Tlatilco (Mexico). National Museum of Anthropology, Mexico City. (Ph. U.M. Alama).*

14 *Culture of western Mexico (4th-8th centuries?) Pottery jar representing a fantastic animal. Provenance unknown. Height 20.5 cm; width 17.5 cm. National Museum of Anthropology, Mexico City. (Ph. U.M. Alama).*

15 *Culture of western Mexico (4th–8th centuries?) Male figure carrying a small human head slung over his shoulder. Pottery. (Front view). Provenance unknown. Height 34 cm; width 21 cm. National Museum of Anthropology, Mexico City. (Ph. U.M. Alama).*

16 *Culture of western Mexico (4th-8th centuries?) Jar representing a stylised bird. Red polished pottery, with black spots; beak and eyes light yellow. From Colima? Height 16.3 cm; length 29.8 cm. National Museum of Anthropology, Mexico City. (Ph. U.M. Alama).*

17 *Cf. No. 15: front view.*

18 *Culture of western Mexico (4th-8th centuries?) Effigy jar. Pottery. A kneeling hunter carrying a deer on his shoulders. From Colima? Height 17.8 cm; width 17 cm. Dumbarton Oaks, Washington. (Ph. Museum).*

19 *Culture of western Mexico (4th-8th centuries?) Mortar with three feet. Pottery with black slip, and remains of polychrome "cloisonné" decoration in a technique resembling that of Teotihuacán. From Jiquilpan (Michoacán). Height 12 cm; greatest diameter 36 cm. View of outside. National Museum of Anthropology, Mexico City. (Ph. U.M. Alama).*

20 *Culture of western Mexico (4th-8th centuries?) Pottery cup, with polished red slip and black and white geometric decoration. From Chupícuaro (Guanajuato). Height 12.5 cm; diameter 19 cm. National Museum of Anthropology, Mexico City. (Ph. U.M. Alama).*

21 *Culture of western Mexico (4th-8th centuries?) Stirrup-spouted jar in the form of a human head. Pottery. From Colima. Height 26 cm; width 17.5 cm. National Museum of Anthropology, Mexico City. (Ph. U.M. Alama).*

22 *Culture of western Mexico (4th-8th centuries?) Tripod jar. Pottery. From Chupícuaro (Guanajuato). Height 15.5 cm; length 28.5 cm. National Museum of Anthropology, Mexico City. (Ph. U.M. Alama).*

23 *Culture of western Mexico (4th-8th centuries?) Mortar with three feet. Pottery. From Chupícuaro (Guanajuato). Height 12 cm; width 20 cm. National Museum of Anthropology, Mexico City. (Ph. U.M. Alama).*

24 *Culture of western Mexico (4th-8th centuries?) Zoomorphic double jar. Pottery. From Chupícuaro (Guanajuato). Height (to heads) 12 cm; width 15 cm; length 22.5 cm. National Museum of Anthropology, Mexico City. (Ph. U.M. Alama).*

25 *Culture of western Mexico (4th-8th centuries?) Phytomorphic jar. Pottery, with traces of negative decoration in lower part. From Colima- Height 20 cm; greatest diameter 29.5 cm. National Museum of Anthro· pology, Mexico City. (Ph. U.M. Alama).*

26 *Culture of western Mexico (4th-8th centuries?) Zoomorphic figurine. Pottery, painted red and polished, with black dots and incised lines From Colima? Height 21 cm; length 32.5 cm; width 22.2 cm. Nationat Museum of Anthropology, Mexico City. (Ph. U.M. Alama).*

27 *Culture of western Mexico (4th-8th centuries?) Tripod jar, with fee. in the form of parrots. Pottery, with polished reddish slip. From Colima. Height 21 cm; greatest diameter 13.5 cm. National Museum of Anthropology, Mexico City. (Ph. U.M. Alama).*

28 *Olmec culture (1st century B.C. to 2nd century A.D.) The Kunz Axe, a ceremonial axe in jade. Height 27.9 cm. American Museum of Natural History, New York. (Ph. Museum).*

29 *Teotihuacán culture (3rd-7th centuries) Pottery figurine. Body modelled, head made in mould. Provenance unknown. Height 11 cm. National Museum of Anthropology, Mexico City. (Ph. U.M. Alama).*

30 *Teotihuacán culture (3rd-7th centuries) Anthropomorphic figurine. Pottery. Provenance unknown. Height 9 cm. National Museum of Anthropology, Mexico City. (Ph. U.M. Alama).*

31 *Teotihuacán culture (3rd-7th centuries) Anthropomorphic figurine of an old man, probably the fire god. From San Miguel Azcapotzalco (Federal District). Height 16.1 cm; width 10.3 cm. National Museum of Anthropology, Mexico City. (Ph. U.M. Alama).*

32 *Teotihuacán culture (3rd-7th centuries) Pottery figurine. Made in mould, with applied* (pastillage) *decoration. Provenance unknown. Height*

17 cm; greatest width 13 cm. National Museum of Anthropology, Mexico City. (Ph. U.M. Alama).

33 *Teotihuacán culture (3rd-7th centuries) Pottery figurine of the "Fat God". Height 17 cm; width 13 cm. Provenance unknown. National Museum of Anthropology, Mexico City. (Ph. U.M. Alama).*

34 *Olmec culture (1st century B.C. to 2nd century A.D.) The Tuxtla Statuette. Jadeite. Hieroglyphic inscription. Veracruz. Smithsonian Institution, Washington. (Ph. Museum).*

35 *Olmec culture (1st century B.C. to 2nd century A.D.) Standing figure of a jaguar. Serpentine. Height 7.8 cm. Dumbarton Oaks, Washington (Robert Woods Bliss Collection). (Ph. Museum).*

36 *Teotihuacán culture (3rd-7th centuries) Shell decorated in fresco with motifs and hieroglyphs relating to the water god. From Teotihuacán Length 36 cm; greatest width 19.8 cm. National Museum of Anthropology Mexico City. (Ph. U.M. Alama).*

37 *Teotihuacán culture (3rd-7th centuries) Jar decorated in fresco or "pseudo-cloisonné" technique representing a priest in a feather headdress holding a maize plant. Provenance unknown. Height 9 cm; greatest diameter 12.5 cm. National Museum of Anthropology, Mexico City. (Ph. U.M. Alama).*

38 *Teotihuacán culture (3rd-7th centuries) Jar. Beige pottery. From La Ventilla, Teotihuacán. Height 10.8 cm; greatest diameter 14.4 cm. National Museum of Anthropology, Mexico City. (Ph. U.M. Alama).*

39 *Teotihuacán culture (3rd-7th centuries) Tripod jar, with incised decoration representing the rain god Tlaloc; remains of painting in red and black. From Teotihuacán. Height 13 cm; greatest diameter 13.2 cm. National Museum of Anthropology, Mexico City. (Ph. U.M. Alama).*

40 *Teotihuacán culture (3rd-7th centuries) Tripod jar decorated with agricultural motifs in fresco. Provenance unknown. Height 13 cm; greatest diameter 13.5 cm. National Museum of Anthropology, Mexico City. (Ph. U.M. Alama).*

41 *Teotihuacán: Pyramid of the Sun. (Ph. J. Soustelle).*

42 *Teotihuacán culture (3rd-7th centuries) Figurine, perhaps representing the fire god. Provenance unknown. Height 12 cm. National Museum of Anthropology, Mexico City. (Ph. U.M. Alama).*

43 *Teotihuacán culture (3rd-7th centuries) Pottery mask. From Teotihuacán. Height 9.5 cm; width 17.3 cm. National Museum of Anthropology, Mexico City. (Ph. U.M. Alama).*

44 *Teotihuacán culture (3rd-7th centuries) Two anthropomorphic figurines, one of them representing a hunchback. Pottery; the heads are made in a mould and the bodies modelled. Provenance unknown. Greatest height 7.4 cm; width 4.7 cm; length 10.8 cm. National Museum of Anthropology, Mexico City. (Ph. U.M. Alama).*

45 *Olmec culture (1st century B.C. to 2nd century A.D.) Mask or helmet representing a jaguar. Brown marble. Olmec style? Probably from Rio Balsas (Guerrero). Height 12.9 cm; width 17.6 cm. Dumbarton Oaks, Washington. (Ph. Museum).*

46 *Teotihuacán culture (3rd-7th centuries) Hemispherical jar. Light beige pottery. Engraved decoration showing richly dressed figures, eagles and coyotes. From tomb at Las Colinas, Calpulalpan (Mexico). Height 7.5 cm; greatest diameter 13.5 cm. National Museum of Anthropology, Mexico City. (Ph. U.M. Alama).*

47 *Teotihuacán culture (3rd-7th centuries) Moulded figurine of a priest. Provenance unknown. Height 14.4 cm; greatest width 16.5 cm. National Museum of Anthropology, Mexico City. (Ph. U.M. Alama).*

48 *Teotihuacán culture (3rd-7th centuries). The Teotihuacán "Cross", an architectural element representing the rain god Tlaloc. Basalt, with traces of red paint. 151 × 145 cm. Teotihuacán area. Regional Museum, Teotihuacán. (Ph. Museum).*

49 *Teotihuacán: Tepantitlán, fresco representing a priest of Tlaloc. (Ph. H. Lehmann).*

50 *Teotihuacán culture (3rd-7th centuries) Pottery mask representing a human head emerging from a bird's beak. Provenance unknown. Greatest height 11.3 cm; width 11.1 cm. National Museum of Anthropology, Mexico City. (Ph. U.M. Alama).*

51 *Teotihuacán culture (3rd-7th centuries) Stone mask. From San Angel road. Height 22.3 cm; width 28.2 cm. National Museum of Anthropology, Mexico City. (Ph. U.M. Alama).*

52 *Teotihuacán culture (3rd-7th centuries) Mask in black volcanic stone. From Teotihuacán. Height 14 cm; width 13 cm. National Museum of Anthropology, Mexico City. (Ph. U.M. Alama).*

53 *Teotihuacán culture (3rd-7th centuries) Diorite mask. From Teotihuacán (Zone 4, Avenue of the Dead). Height 16.1 cm; width 15.9 cm. National Museum of Anthropology, Mexico City. (Ph. U.M. Alama).*

54 *Teotihuacán: Tetitla, fresco. (Ph. H. Lehmann).*

55 *Teotihuacán culture (3rd-7th centuries) Fragment of hollow figurine. Light beige pottery, modelled. From Teotihuacán. Greatest height 15.3 cm; greatest width 19.8 cm. National Museum of Anthropology, Mexico City. (Ph. U.M. Alama).*

56 *Palenque: the Palace. Stucco bas-relief. (Ph. J. Soustelle).*

57 *Palenque: the Palace. Stucco decoration on east front. (Ph. J. Soustelle).*

58–59 *Palenque: the Palace. Bas-reliefs of archaic or archaistic style representing slaves or prisoners in an attitude of supplication. (Ph. J. Soustelle).*

60 *Palenque: the Palace, with restoration work in progress. (Ph. J. Soustelle).*

61 *Palenque: Temple of the Inscriptions. (Ph. J. Soustelle).*

62 *Palenque. On the left, Temple of the Inscriptions; on the right, the Palace. (Ph. J. Soustelle).*

63 *Palenque: Temple of the Sun. (Ph. J. Soustelle).*

64 *Palenque: general view of the three temples. Left, Temple of the Foliated Cross; centre, Temple of the Cross; right, Temple of the Sun. (Ph. J. Soustelle).*

65 *Classic Maya culture (3rd-9th centuries) Stucco head from crypt of Temple of the Inscriptions, Palenque. (Front view). National Museum of Anthropology, Mexico City. (Ph. Museum).*

66 *The same: side view.*

67 *Classic Maya culture (3rd-9th centuries) The Leyden Plate. Jadeite. Probably from Tikal area (Guatemala). Obverse: chief standing on a captive. Early period (4th century). Rijksmuseum voor Volkenkunde, Leyden. (Ph. Museum).*

68 *The same. Reverse: hieroglyphs indicating the date 320 A.D.*

69–70 *Classic Maya culture (3rd-9th centuries) Carved wood from Tikal (Guatemala). Museum für Völkerkunde, Basle. (Ph. Museum).*

71 *Classic Maya culture (3rd-9th centuries) Bowl. Onyx marble. Probably from state of Campeche. Late period. Height 11.6 cm. Dumbarton Oaks, Washington. (Ph. Museum).*

72 *Classic Maya culture (3rd-9th centuries) Polychrome jar. From Chamá (Guatemala). University Museum of Pennsylvania. (Ph. Museum).*

73 *Uxmal: Governor's Palace. Main front: a Maya false vault. (Ph. H. Lehmann).*

74 *Classic Maya culture (3rd-9th centuries) Effigy whistle representing an old man and a girl. Pottery. Jaina style, late period. Height 25.6 cm; width 13.5 cm. Dumbarton Oaks, Washington. (Ph. Museum).*

75 *Classic Maya culture (3rd-9th centuries) Effigy whistle representing a woman. Moulded, with applied* (pastillage) *decoration. From Tomb 351, Jaina (Campeche). Height 19.4 cm; width 11.9 cm. National Museum of Anthropology, Mexico City. (Ph. U.M. Alama).*

76 *Classic Maya culture (3rd-9th centuries) Effigy bell. Moulded, with applied* (pastillage) *decoration. From Tomb 143, Jaina (Campeche). Height 17 cm; width 12 cm. National Museum of Anthropology, Mexico City. (Ph. U.M. Alama).*

77 *Classic Maya culture (3rd-9th centuries) Anthropomorphic figurine. Moulded; much restored. From Jaina (Campeche). Height 19 cm; width 10.1 cm. National Museum of Anthropology, Mexico City. (Ph. U.M. Alama).*

78 *Classic Maya culture (3rd-9th centuries) Moulded anthropomorphic figurine holding an incense pouch in the left hand. Horizontal scarifications on the face. Restored. From Campeche? Height 23.8 cm; width 12.2 cm. National Museum of Anthropology, Mexico City. (Ph. U.M. Alama).*

79 *Classic Maya culture (3rd-9th centuries) Effigy whistle: a seated figure with closed eyes, perhaps representing a dead man. From Campeche. Height 10.3 cm; width 6.5 cm. National Museum of Anthropology, Mexico City. (Ph. U.M. Alama).*

80 *Classic Maya culture (3rd-9th centuries) Effigy whistle. From Jaina (Campeche). Height 13.7 cm; width 10 cm. National Museum of Anthropology, Mexico City. (Ph. U.M. Alama).*

81 *Classic Maya culture (3rd-9th centuries) Effigy whistle representing a dwarf. Light beige pottery. From Jaina (Campeche). Height 10.7 cm; width 5.3 cm. National Museum of Anthropology, Mexico City. (Ph. U.M. Alama).*

82 *Classic Maya culture (3rd-9th centuries) Effigy bell: a figure with an elaborate hair style, ear ornaments, a belt tied in front and a garment reaching to the ankles. Restored. Provenance unknown. Height 17.5 cm. National Museum of Anthropology, Mexico City. (Ph. U.M. Alama).*

83 *Classic Maya culture (3rd-9th centuries) Effigy whistle. Pottery. Jaina style, late period. Height 20.6 cm; width 12.2 cm. Dumbarton Oaks, Washington (Robert Woods Bliss Collection). (Ph. Museum).*

84 *Classic Maya culture (3rd-9th centuries) Figurine of a woman. Pottery. Jaina style (600-900 A.D.). Height 41.4 cm. Dumbarton Oaks, Washington (Robert Woods Bliss Collection). (Ph. Museum).*

85 *Classic Maya culture (3rd-9th centuries) Flat-bottomed pottery jar of cylindrical shape with decoration in two engraved panels. From Uxmal (Yucatán). National Museum of Anthropology, Mexico City. (Ph. U.M. Alama).*

86 *Classic Maya culture (3rd-9th centuries) Human head, with marked cranial deformation. Modelled stucco. From Palenque (Chiapas). Length 11 cm; width 16.4 cm. National Museum of Anthropology, Mexico City. (Ph. U.M. Alama).*

87 *Classic Maya culture (3rd-9th centuries) Effigy whistle: a woman, seated, with a child. Made in mould, with applied* (pastillage) *decoration. From Tomb 227, Jaina (Campeche). Height 13.1 cm; width 7 cm. National Museum of Anthropology, Mexico City. (Ph. U.M. Alama).*

88 *Zapotec culture (3rd-10th centuries) Pottery statuette, hollow. Very untypical of Zapotec work; similar to the large hollow pottery statuettes of Veracruz. Provenance unknown. Height 66.5 cm; width 42 cm. National Museum of Anthropology, Mexico City. (Ph. U.M. Alama).*

89 *Classic Maya culture (3rd-9th centuries) Face of the sun god. Modelled stucco; painted red. From Palenque (Chiapas). Height 22 cm; width 10 cm. National Museum of Anthropology, Mexico City. (Ph. U.M. Alama).*

90 *Zapotec culture (3rd-10th centuries) Ceremonial jar representing the goddess "13 Serpent". From Tomb 103, Monte Albán (Oaxaca). Height 37 cm; width 31 cm. National Museum of Anthropology, Mexico City. (Ph. U.M. Alama).*

91 *Zapotec culture (3rd-10th centuries) Jar representing the rain god Cocijo. From Tlalixtac (Oaxaca). Height 19.5 cm; width 12.5 cm. National Museum of Anthropology, Mexico City. (Ph. U.M. Alama).*

92 *Zapotec culture (3rd-10th centuries) Pottery urn. From Silacayoapan (Oaxaca). Height 25.5 cm. National Museum of Anthropology, Mexico City. (Ph. U.M. Alama).*

93 *Zapotec culture (3rd-10th centuries) Ceremonial urn. Pottery. From Cuilapan (Oaxaca). Height 23.5 cm; greatest width 18.3 cm. National Museum of Anthropology, Mexico City. (Ph. U.M. Alama).*

94 *Zapotec culture ((3rd-10th centuries) Ceremonial urn representing the god with the glyph "L", who was associated with the bat and with the maize cult. Pottery. From Monte Albán. Height 23 cm; width 30 cm. National Museum of Anthropology, Mexico City. (Ph. U.M. Alama).*

95 *Zapotec culture (3rd-10th centuries) Ceremonial urn representing a divinity with a feathered headdress and filed teeth. Provenance unknown. Height 32 cm; width 32.3 cm. National Museum of Anthropology, Mexico City. (Ph. U.M. Alama).*

96 *Zapotec culture (3rd-10th centuries) Fragment of pottery urn. From Oaxaca valley. Height 36 cm. National Museum of Anthropology, Mexico City. (Ph. U.M. Alama).*

97 *Zapotec culture (3rd-10th centuries) Funerary urn. Pottery. A figure wearing a loincloth made of leaves, with a headdress of 7 heads of maize. Represents a maize god known to the Aztecs as Chicomollotzin (from* chicome, *seven, and* ollotl, *head of grain, with the reverential suffix* tzin*). Height 61.7 cm. From Oaxaca. Musée de l'Homme, Paris. (Ph. Museum).*

98 *Zapotec culture (3rd-10th centuries) Ceremonial jar representing the serpent-faced god. Pottery. Hieroglyph in the hair. From Tlacochahuaya, district of Tlacolula (Oaxaca). Height 32 cm; width 22 cm. National Museum of Anthropology, Mexico City. (Ph. U.M. Alama).*

99 *Zapotec culture (3rd-10th centuries) Ceremonial urn representing the rain god Cocijo. From Ejutla (Oaxaca). Height 32 cm. National Museum of Anthropology, Mexico City. (Ph. U.M. Alama).*

100 *Zapotec culture (3rd–10th centuries) Anthropomorphic urn. Pottery. Hieroglyph on pectoral. From Tomb 103, Monte Albán. Height 34.5 cm; width 24 cm. National Museum of Anthropology, Mexico City. (Ph. U.M. Alama).*

101 *Gulf Coast culture (7th-10th centuries) Remojadas: head of warrior. Pottery. Veracruz. American Museum of Natural History, New York. (Ph. Museum).*

102 *Gulf Coast culture (7th-10th centuries)* Palma *representing a pelican. Andesite. Provenance unknown. Height 39.5 cm; width 9 cm; thickness 16.5 cm. National Museum of Anthropology, Mexico City. (Ph. U.M. Alama).*

103 *Gulf Coast culture (7th-10th centuries)* Palma *representing a human head. Basalt. (Three-quarter-face view from right). Provenance unknown. Height 17.5 cm; width 11.5 cm. National Museum of Anthropology, Mexico City. (Ph. U.M. Alama).*

104 *The same: back view.*

105 *The same: three-quarter-face view from left.*

106 *Gulf Coast culture (7th-10th centuries) Diorite sculpture of the type known as a "votive axe", representing a male head with moustache. (Three-quarter-face view from right). Provenance unknown. Height 26.5 cm; width 19 cm; thickness 4 cm. National Museum of Anthropology, Mexico City. (Ph. U.M. Alama).*

107 *The same: three-quarter-face view from left.*

108 *El Tajín: the Pyramid. (Ph. J. Soustelle).*

109 *El Tajín: stela of volcanic stone. (Ph. J. Soustelle).*

110 *Gulf Coast culture (7th-10th centuries)* Palma *representing a saurian. Provenance unknown. Height 52.5 cm; width 22.5 cm; thickness 13 cm. National Museum of Anthropology, Mexico City. (Ph. U.M. Alama).*

111 *The same: another view.*

112 *Gulf Coast culture (7th-10th centuries) Onyx sculpture of the "votive axe" type representing a human skull. (Three-quarter-face view). Provenance unknown. Height 19.5 cm; width 6 cm; thickness 16.5 cm. National Museum of Anthropology, Mexico City. (Ph. U.M. Alama).*

113 *The same: profile view.*

114 *Gulf Coast culture (7th-10th centuries) Pottery jars. Isla de los Sacrificios. Late period. British Museum. (Ph. Museum).*

115 *Gulf Coast culture (7th-10th centuries) Dish with decoration in two colours representing a stylised rodent. Provenance unknown. Height 4.5 cm; greatest diameter 18 cm. National Museum of Anthropology, Mexico City. (Ph. U.M. Alama).*

116 *Gulf Coast culture (7th-10th centuries) Pottery jar with geometric and symbolic motifs. Provenance unknown. Height 10 cm; greatest width 18.7 cm. National Museum of Anthropology, Mexico City. (Ph. U.M. Alama).*

117 *Gulf Coast culture (7th-10th centuries) Jar in orange-coloured pottery with polychrome decoration. From Isla de los Sacrificios (Veracruz). Height 24 cm; greatest diameter 12 cm. National Museum of Anthropology, Mexico City. (Ph. U.M. Alama).*

118 *Gulf Coast culture (7th-10th centuries) Remojadas: seated figurine. Rijksmuseum voor Volkenkunde, Leyden. (Ph. Museum).*

119 *Gulf Coast culture (7th-10th centuries) Figurine with smiling face and filed teeth. Pottery. From central Veracruz. Height 42 cm; width 20 cm. National Museum of Anthropology, Mexico City. (Ph. U.M. Alama).*

120 *Gulf Coast culture (7th-10th centuries) Effigy whistle representing a woman with filed teeth. Pottery. From El Faisán (Veracruz). Height 33.7 cm; width 20 cm. National Museum of Anthropology, Mexico City. (Ph. U.M. Alama).*

121 *Gulf Coast culture (7th-10th centuries) Head with filed teeth. Pottery. From Las Mecillas, commune of Cosamaloapan (Veracruz). Height 18 cm; width 17.5 cm. National Museum of Anthropology, Mexico City. (Ph. U.M. Alama).*

122 *Gulf Coast culture (7th-10th centuries) Figurine of a smiling man, lying prone. Pottery. Provenance unknown. Height 12 cm; length 23.5 cm. National Museum of Anthropology, Mexico City. (Ph. U.M. Alama).*

123–124 *Gulf Coast culture (7th-10th centuries) Remojadas: seated figurines. Rijksmuseum voor Volkenkunde, Leyden. (Ph. Museum).*

125 *Chichén Itzá: Chacmool in Temple of the Warriors. (Ph. J. Soustelle).*

126 *Chichén Itzá: general view of Temple of the Warriors. (Ph. J. Soustelle).*

127 *Toltec-Maya culture (10th-13th centuries) Chased gold disc with scene of human sacrifice. Chichén Itzá. Peabody Museum. (Ph. Museum).*

128 *Toltec-Maya culture (10th-13th centuries) Chased gold disc showing a naval battle between Mayas and Toltecs. Chichén Itzá. Peabody Museum. (Ph. Museum).*

129 *Toltec-Maya culture (10th-13th centuries) Chased gold disc with figures of warriors. Chichén Itzá. Peabody Museum. (Ph. Museum).*

130 *Chichén Itzá: in foreground, Caracol; to rear, Temple of Quetzalcoatl. (Ph. J. Soustelle).*

131 *Chichén Itzá: the Ball Court. (Ph. J. Soustelle).*

132 *Tula: Chacmool. (Ph. H. Lehmann).*

133 *Tula: frieze on Coatepantli ("Serpent Wall"). (Ph. H. Lehmann).*

134 *Tulum: Temple of the Frescoes. Detail of a fresco. (Ph. H. Lehmann).*

135 *Tula: caryatid, Temple of the Morning Star. (Ph. Musée de l'Homme).*

136 *Mixtec culture (?) Gold bell. Hermitage Museum, Leningrad. (Ph. Museum).*

137 *Mixteca-Puebla culture (13th-16th centuries) Mexican calendar of the 15th century, known as the* Bologna *or* Cospi Codex. *On this page the archer god of the dawn is shown hitting other divinities with his arrows. Library of Bologna University. (Ph. Cav. Luigi D'Aurizio).*

138 *Mixteca-Puebla culture (13th-16th centuries) Page 70 of the* Zouche-Nuttall Codex, *with the warrior "8 Deer" ("Jaguar's Claw") and other characters designated by their hieroglyphic names. British Museum. (Ph. Museum).*

139 *Mixteca-Puebla culture (13th-16th centuries) The* Bologna (Cospi) Codex. *This page shows 65 days of the divinatory calendar, with the guardian divinity for each day. Library of Bologna University. (Ph. Cav. Luigi D'Aurizio).*

140 *Mixteca-Puebla culture (13th-16th centuries) Wooden shield inlaid with turquoise mosaic. Late post-classic period. Puebla. Diameter 31.7 cm. Museum of the American Indian, New York. (Ph. Museum).*

141 *Mixteca-Puebla culture (13th-16th centuries) Pottery head of the god Xipe Totec, with the skin of a flayed victim covering his face. Provenance unknown. Height 17.5 cm; width 13.5 cm. National Museum of Anthropology, Mexico City. (Ph. U.M. Alama).*

142 *Mixtec culture (13th-16th centuries) Tripod jar, of globular shape, decorated with birds and human heads. From Zayacatlán (Oaxaca). Height 22.2 cm; diameter 20 cm. National Museum of Anthropology, Mexico City. (Ph. U.M. Almaa).*

143 *Mixteca-Puebla culture (13th-16th centuries) Tripod jar, of globular shape; polychrome decoration, with stylised motifs similar to those found in the pottery of Nazca (Peru). Provenance unknown. Height 22.2 cm; greatest diameter 13.5 cm. National Museum of Anthropology, Mexico City.(Ph. U.M. Alama).*

144 *Mixtec culture (13th-16th centuries) Painted pottery jar in the form of a roe-deer's head. Mitla (Oaxaca). Musée de l'Homme, Paris. (Ph. Museum).*

145 *Mixteca-Puebla culture (13th-16th centuries) Pottery cup with polychrome decoration. From "Ex-Volador", Mexico City. Height 11 cm; greatest diameter 13.8 cm. National Museum of Anthropology, Mexico City. (Ph. U.M. Alama).*

146 *Mixteca-Puebla culture (13th-16th centuries) Pottery cup. Provenance unknown. Height 14 cm; greatest diameter 19.5 cm. National Museum of Anthropology, Mexico City. (Ph. U.M. Alama).*

147 *Mixteca-Puebla culture (13th-16th centuries) Pottery jar. Provenance unknown. Height 18 cm; greatest diameter 17 cm. National Museum of Anthropology, Mexico City. (Ph. U.M. Alama).*

148 *Mixteca-Puebla culture (13th-16th centuries) Tripod bowl with hollow feet in the form of serpents' heads. Pottery. Inside decorated in polychrome with central motif of six-petalled flower surrounded by Greek keys ending in volutes. Provenance unknown. Height 5.6 cm; diameter 16.2 cm. National Museum of Anthropology, Mexico City. (Ph. U.M. Alama).*

149 *Huaxtec culture (14th-15th centuries) Stone statue. From Pánuco. British Museum. (Ph. Museum).*

150 *Huaxtec culture (14th-15th centuries) Statue with heads facing to front and rear. (Rear view). From Chilitujú. Brooklyn Museum. (Ph. Museum).*

151 *The same: front view.*

152 *Aztec culture (14th-16th centuries) Death's head (*miquiztli*) in rock crystal, representing Mictlantecuhtli, god of death. Probably designed as a pendant, with a vertical suspension hole (bored from both sides with emery-tipped copper drills). Height 11 cm; length 15 cm; weight 2.75 kg. Musée de l'Homme, Paris. (Ph. Museum).*

153 *Aztec culture (14th-16th centuries) Jadeite mask. (Front view). Museum für Völkerkunde, Basle. (Ph. Museum).*

154 *The same: side view.*

155 *Aztec culture (14th-16th centuries) Statue of Xolotl (god of rebirth: one of the forms of Quetzalcoatl, whose characteristic earrings he wears). Jade. The front view, with a skull-like face, represents Death, recalling the myth of the descent into the underworld. Württembergisches Landesmuseum, Stuttgart. (Ph. Museum).*

156 *The same: rear view, with a representation of the solar disc (the symbol of rebirth).*

157 *Aztec or Mixteca-Puebla culture Jadeite statuette of the god Tezcatlipoca. (Front view). The left foot is replaced by a serpent's head; the god's attribute, a mirror, is on his breast. Height 6.7 cm; width 4.2 cm. Musée de l'Homme, Paris. (Ph. Museum).*

158 *The same: three-quarter-face view.*

159 *Aztec culture (14th-16th centuries) Jadeite figurine of a rabbit, seated, with a warrior's head in an eagle helmet in its lap. Height 15.1 cm. Dumbarton Oaks, Washington (Robert Woods Bliss Collection). (Ph. Museum).*

160 *Aztec culture (14th-16th centuries)* Quauhxicalli, *a ceremonial jar of carved stone. British Museum. (Ph. Museum).*

161 *Aztec culture (14th-16th centuries) Jar of hard stone with sculptured face. Museum für Völkerkunde, Vienna. (Ph. Museum).*

162 *Aztec culture (14th-16th centuries) Statue of Xipe Totec. Museum für Völkerkunde, Basle. (Ph. Museum).*

163 *Aztec culture (14th-16th centuries) Stone figure, probably the young goddess of vegetation and flowers, Xochiquetzal. (Front view). Provenance unknown. Height 39 cm. National Museum of Anthropology, Mexico City. (Ph. U.M. Alama).*

164 *The same: three-quarter-face view.*

165 *Aztec culture (14th-16th centuries) Stone figure of a* maceualli *(peasant). Provenance unknown. Height 45 cm. National Museum of Anthropology, Mexico City. (Ph. U.M. Alama).*

166 *Aztec culture (14th-16th centuries) Basalt figure of a* maceualli *(peasant), an old man wearing only a loincloth. (Front view). May have served as a standard-bearer. Provenance unknown. Height 48.5 cm. National Museum of Anthropology, Mexico City. (Ph. U.M. Alama).*

167 *The same: three-quarter-face view.*

168 *Aztec culture (14th-16th centuries) Two-headed serpent. Wood and mosaic. British Museum. (Ph. Museum).*

169 *Aztec culture (14th-16th centuries) Mask of the god Tezcatlipoca. Mottled green stone. Probably from Xochimilco, Valley of Mexico. On the back is carved the date "2 Reed" (1507 A.D.). Height 18.5 cm; width 16.3 cm. Dumbarton Oaks, Washington. (Ph. Museum).*

170 *Aztec culture (14th-16th centuries) Onyx mask. Provenance unknown, Height 21 cm; width 22.5 cm. National Museum of Anthropology. Mexico City. (Ph. U.M. Alama).*

171 *Aztec culture (14th-16th centuries) Mask in beige pottery. From Cholula (Puebla). Height 17 cm; width 17.5 cm. National Museum of Anthropology, Mexico City. (Ph. U.M. Alama).*

172 *Aztec culture (14th-16th centuries)* Teponaztli, *a horizontal wooden gong. British Museum. (Ph. Museum).*

173–174 *Aztec culture (14th-16th centuries) Serpent. Green stone. Height 16 cm; greatest diameter 29 cm. National Museum of Anthropology, Mexico City. (Ph. U.M. Alama).*

175 *Aztec culture (14th-16th centuries) Page 13 of the* Codex Borbonicus, *showing the thirteen days from* ce-ollin, *"1 Motion", to* matlactli-omey-atl, *"13 Water", with the divinities corresponding to each day and night. Library of the National Assembly, Paris. (Ph. Library).*

176 *Aztec culture (14th-16th centuries) Jadeite figurine. British Museum. (Ph. Museum).*

177 *Aztec culture (14th-16th centuries) Large feather headdress, Moctezuma's crown. Museum für Völkerkunde, Vienna. (Ph. Museum).*

178 *Aztec culture (14th-16th centuries) Shield covered with a feather mosaic representing the water monster Ahuitzotl. Museum für Völkerkunde, Vienna. (Ph. Museum).*

179 *Aztec culture (14th-16th centuries)* Atlatl *(javelin-thrower), in wood and chased gold. British Museum. (Ph. Museum).*

180 *Aztec culture (14th-16th centuries) Helmet with two horns. Wood and mosaic. British Museum. (Ph. Museum).*

181 *Aztec culture (14th-16th centuries)* Teponaztli, *a two-toned gong of carved wood, representing a fantastic animal. May date from the period immediately after the Spanish conquest. Provenance unknown. Length 87 cm; width 25.5 cm; greatest height 23 cm. National Museum of Anthropology, Mexico City. (Ph. U.M. Alama).*

182–183 *Aztec culture (14th-16th centuries) Basalt figure of a monkey. Provenance unknown. Height 34 cm. National Museum of Anthropology, Mexico City. (Ph. U.M. Alama).*

184 *Aztec culture (14th-16th centuries) Shield covered with feather mosaic. Württembergisches Landesmuseum, Stuttgart. (Ph. Museum).*

Note "Provenance unknown", in relation to objects not obtained by scientific excavation, indicates that although the culture to which they belong is known the exact place of discovery is not.

PRINTED IN SWITZERLAND

INDEX

Printed in Switzerland

THE TEXT AND ILLUSTRATIONS
IN THIS VOLUME WERE PRINTED
ON THE PRESSES OF NAGEL PUBLISHERS
IN GENEVA.

FINISHED IN JUNE 1967.
BINDING BY NAGEL PUBLISHERS,
GENEVA.

PLATES ENGRAVED BY CLICHÉS UNION, PARIS

LEGAL DEPOSIT No. 427

PRINTED IN SWITZERLAND

Casas Grandes
Guasave
Chalchihuites
La Quemada
Rio
Lerma
NAYARIT
JALISC
MICHOA
COLIMA
Tzintz
0 65 130 325 520 650 Km